POLISH COO

200+ AUTHENTIC RECIPES INCLUDING GOULASH, GOLABI̶ ̶ ̶ ̶ ̶ ̶IE,
AND OTHER TRADITIONAL POLISH COMFORT FOODS

TABLE OF CONTENTS

HISTORY OF POLAND

Poland is an essential part of the European continent. This ninth largest country is surrounded by the forests from the northwestern parts of Europe, seas of the Atlantic Ocean, and the fertile planes of the European and Asian frontiers. Don't forget the lakes; Europe's largest lake districts are here.

Poland is an all-in-one weather country as three types of weather conditions influence the country's climate. The oceanic air blows from the west, the cold air from the Scandinavian countries or Russia, and the warmer air from the south. In winter, the weather gets colder and crisp due to the polar air and, in the mid-summer, the weather becomes warmer and dry due to the subtropical air; but in the late summer and autumn, this air brings pleasant days for its people.

The variety of ethnic communities was Poland's popularity before World War II. Apart from the ethnic Polish community, Ukrainians, Jews, and Belarusians were the largest. These people were dispersed in different areas of the country, and the war was fatal for the population and the ethnic communities in Poland. At the moment, Poland has around 38 million inhabitants.

Before World War 2, this country was known for agriculture and mining. However, during the communist rule, Poland developed an industrial sector for running the state economy. From the mid-1970s, the country's economic growth slowed down, and then in the 1980s, hyperinflation ruined the country's economic structure. This continued until the 1990s, when the scale of inflation began to fall. In 2000 the inflation rate fell to 10% from 250% in 1990. Ups and downs were prevalent until 2014 when the country's economy started stabilizing.

Agriculture is an enormous part of the Polish economy. This makes a great interpretation of the Polish eating routine, with oat grains like wheat, rye, grain, and buckwheat making up the staples of the eating regimen. Similarly, different items like potatoes, cucumbers, mushrooms, cabbage, and beetroots are well-known. Potatoes are the most convenient side dish found at a Polish dinner.

ORIGIN OF POLISH FOOD

Poland is situated at the intersection of shipping lanes between Europe and Asia. Dealers from inaccessible terrains came to Poland for gold and exchanged colorful flavors and extraordinary culinary thoughts.

Various impacts have made Polish food exceptionally wealthy in flavors. It is not hard to track down hints of Jewish food's oriental, sweet, and hot taste. The Lithuanians showed the polish people the unique specialty of dry-preserving meat, giving them dried franks, for example, kindziuk.

Like the Ukrainians, the polish people love to eat dumplings. French cooking has impacted the heavenly treats of Poland. The local food of Poland is a flavorful mix of traditional and modern customs. Polish people have consistently had great natural items, such as Polish salt, which comes from the renowned mines in Wieliczka and Bochnia close to Kraków.

Verifiably, Polish timberlands have been plentiful in wild game and were home to nectar, creating honey bees. This made Polish food wealthy in honey, and Polish nectar was a sought-after item all through Europe. Today, nectar making is encountering a renaissance, and numerous fantastic enormous beehives produce the nectar of remarkable quality in an assortment of flavors. It is generally presented with curds and cottage cheese.

Nature's bounty is evident in much of Polish cooking. The most commonly used cereals are wheat and rye, which have been used for baking fantastic Polish pieces of bread for centuries. Their recipes are also known for using fish. A wide assortment of vegetables was added to the Polish table by Italy born Polish sovereign Bona Sforza. They are served crude as a plate of mixed greens or bubbled and finished with breadcrumbs caramelized in margarine. Our accomplishment,

10

notwithstanding, is the excellent choice of soups which are usually more than 200 varieties. Cucumber pickles are one of the most loved dishes of Polish food. Today, young cooks are mixing the traditional and ancient practices of Polish food with contemporary culinary patterns, making innovative however traditional Polish flavors.

POLISH CUISINE AND TRADITIONS

Polish cuisine has emerged as the most important and healthy cuisine in Europe. Polish cuisine is different from other European cuisines because pickles are an essential part of their meal. There are various exotic flavors in Polish cuisine, such as the sharp taste of mustard plants and the yummy taste of fermented baked goods.

The most famous Polish food, pierogi, needs no presentation of any kind. It appears that pierogi ruskie, or the adored dumplings loaded down with potatoes and cheddar, are perhaps the most famous assortments both in Poland and abroad. Pierogi with meat fillings is the mainstream dish that includes pork, ham meat, chicken, and veal, frequently added with bacon. More refined variants accompany sheep, duck, or goose meat.

Many people are interested in Polish recipes simply because they offer a unique food experience. Polish cuisine is a rich blend of various types of food originating from multicultural influences. The result is a delicious stew of culinary tastes and unique tastes in one dish.

Many ethnic groups throughout history have created jealously guarded dishes that have withstood time and are still popular today. As it turns out, Polish recipes are the best because they are delicious and easy to prepare. The richness of the flavors and the way you can bond with your family while making such a dish make this type of cuisine special.

You may taste a hint of spicy sweetness in some Polish dishes from the influence of Jewish cuisine—Poles dry-cured meat like sausages, as the Lithuanians taught them.

Their love of dumplings came from Ukrainians. Their desserts owe some of their exquisite taste to French cuisine.

The cuisine of Poland is a beautiful blend of peasant and noble traditions alike. They have helpful local ingredients, many of which can be found or substituted for in other countries.

In this cookbook, you will find over 200 recipes that are both tasty and easy to follow. The ingredients used are simple, everyday items found in every household you use day after day. They can be made quickly and easily, giving you more time to spend with your family after work.

You can prepare Polish food at home by learning the list of various ingredients that you will need to start cooking. There are several health benefits of making exquisite cuisine at home, and you will learn about all of them when you read this excellent book.

Following are some interesting facts about Polish food:

Polish food is quite possibly the most delectable cooking style in Europe and worldwide. Polish food is ideal for individuals who desire comfort food sources. Conventional Polish food is elementary to make, and it tastes undoubtedly tasty.

Polish food was dependent on wheat, meat, natural products, spices, nectar, and flavors in medieval times. Everything was available nearby and outgrew Polish soil. In those times, Polish food was very zesty and calorific.

Meat, fish, and vegetables were protected with salt or the sun-drying cycle. The polish people often utilized maturation and pickling techniques also. During the partitions, many additions of other countries influenced Polish cuisine. Finally, Polish food is the effect of the best cooking traditions of neighboring nations.

The word bar does not mean something very similar to a bar in other countries in Poland. Usually, it is a modest milk bar that offers conventional Polish dishes. If you are searching for smooth thin soups, Poland is not the spot for you as practically all traditional soups are relatively thick in texture. Along these lines, when requesting the supper of the day at a sound bar or eatery, you will no doubt get one of many Polish soups.

It can be said that most Polish individuals are obsessed with thoroughly salted cucumbers and cabbage. When the season for these vegetables starts, you can see individuals getting them in massive amounts and starting to consummate their pickling procedure.

Some dishes can be known as the most acclaimed gems in the culinary crown of Poland. Typically, the recipes for these dishes have been passed down from one age to another. A portion of the dishes come from the imperial courts, idealized by notable and regarded culinary specialists. The more excellent parts of them, nonetheless, are dishes eaten by the commoners and are presently connected with the people custom of Poland.

After getting to know these interesting facts, you would surely want to try Polish food as soon as possible.

PREPARING POLISH FOOD AT HOME

Polish food is served in significant portions. Polish cuisine primarily consists of vegetables, grains, mushrooms, and meat.

There is always an extra serving of sauce, butter, and sour cream in Polish cuisine added to almost every served meal.

Polish cuisine has mastered the unique art of blending two unlikely ingredients in the most delicious way possible.

Mostly fried or stewed ingredients are used in Polish dishes so that you can sense a deep and heavenly delicious taste in their meals.

During the middle-ages, herbs, wheat, meat, fruits, and spices were the main components of Polish meals. Every ingredient they used was local, and they grew or produced it on their soil. Polish food was caloric at those times, and they liked to eat spicy food. Also, Polish people enjoyed a lot of local beer and used their hands instead of utensils.

The essence of Polish foods is linked to the country's location and its relationship with its neighbors as well. Polish people love and respect local wild mushrooms and forest fruits. At that time, there was a very popular hunting tradition throughout the region, and it was famous in Poland.

The meat, fish, and vegetables were preserved with salt, and they used the sun drying process as well. Polish people also adopted the fermentation and pickling processes a long time ago.

At the partition, the merging of countries and regions affected Polish cuisine. This is how, in the end, it can be said that Polish food is the product of many cooking traditions reflected by the diversity of its people.

Food lovers know that Polish people are completely obsessed with pickling their cucumbers and cabbage with perfection. People buy these vegetables in bulk when they are in season and then perfect their picking techniques.

Sauerkraut is shredded and pickled cabbage, which is a Polish specialty. Sauerkraut is considered spoiled food in some countries, But Polish people disagree with this theory. They rather enjoy a range of sour delicacies. Sauerkraut is a common ingredient in many traditional Polish dishes.

Apart from pickled cabbage, pickled cucumbers are also served at major gatherings. Pickled cucumbers are always served at any party or family dinner. Pickled cucumbers and Bigos (hunter's stew) are famous appetizers served with chilled vodka. You can even witness this tradition in pubs where they serve drinks with appetizers.

The list of Polish gems isn't limited to just the pickled cucumbers and cabbage. It is much bigger than that. Many dishes are considered the crown holder in the kingdom of Polish cuisine. Most of the dishes are passed from generation to generation. However, many of the dishes have been perfected at the royal courts. The culinary experts perfected these dishes there. Most of the famous dishes are enjoyed by the common people, and they have now become part of the folk tradition of Poland.

Meal arranging and preparing are magnificent abilities to have in your health and fitness toolbox. A thoroughly examined dinner plan can assist you with improving your eating regimen quality or achieving a particular wellbeing objective while setting aside time and cash on the way.

Cooking your meal at home can help you save more time and achieve a good health status. Numerous individuals are extremely busy in their everyday schedules that they do not get enough time to cook at home and eventually eat unhealthy food.

POTATO AND KIELBASA EGG SCRAMBLE

Preparation time: 10min
Cooking time: 25 min

Servings: 4

Ingredients:

- 8 Eggs
- Black pepper
- Salt
- 3 tbsp. Oil
- 1 Onion
- 3 oz. Potatoes
- 6 oz. Polish Kielbasa
- 1/2 cup Parsley, chopped
- 2 oz. Cheese

Directions:

1. In a bowl, whisk 1 tbsp: water, eggs, and ½ tsp. of each black pepper and salt.
2. In a skillet, add 2 tbsp—oil and turn on medium heat. Add potatoes. Cook for about 8 minutes covered. Add onions, cook for 5 minutes.
3. Add kielbasa. Cook 5 minutes.
4. Transfer the mixture to a plate.
5. Add the eggs to the skillet. Cook stirring for 3 minutes. Fold in the kielbasa mixture of parsley and cheese.
6. Serve and enjoy!

POLISH BREAKFAST CEREAL

Preparation time: 5min
Cooking time: 15min

Servings: 2-5

Ingredients:

- 2 tbsp. Sugar (or to taste)
- 2 tbsp. Flour
- ¼ tsp. Vanilla extract
- 1 ½ cup Milk
- 1 Egg
- 1/8 tsp. Salt

Directions:

1. In a bowl, crack one egg and add 1/8 tsp Salt.
2. Whisk well.
3. Now add the flour in the egg but 1 tbsp at a time. Make sure to mix so that you get a homogenous mixture. Add vanilla extract.
4. Pour milk into a small pot. Turn on medium heat. Once simmering, add sugar and stir to dissolve it.
5. Use a spoon to drizzle the egg mixture in the milk. Stir while drizzling—Cook for just 1 minute.
6. Serve and enjoy!

WHITE BORSCHT

Preparation time: 10min
Cooking time: 50min

Servings: 4

Ingredients:

- 1 lb. Kielbasa, smoked
- 6 cups of water
- One leek, sliced
- 2 tbsp. Butter, unsalted
- 1 Onion, sliced
- 3 Garlic cloves, minced
- 2 Potatoes, diced (peeled)
- Two bay leaves
- 1 tsp. Marjoram (this is optional)
- 1 cup of sour cream

- 1 tbsp. Flour
- Black pepper and salt to taste
- 2 tbsp. Dill, chopped
- 2 tbsp. Horseradish
- 1 tbsp. Parsley, chopped
- 4 Eggs, hard-boiled, sliced into wedges

Directions:

1. In a saucepan, add water and the kielbasa. Turn on medium-high heat. Once boiling, reduce to medium-low. Cook 20 minutes.
2. Pour into a large bowl and set aside.
3. Add butter, garlic, onion, and leek in the same saucepan. Cook over medium until soft, 5 minutes. Pour the reserved liquid and add the bay leaf, marjoram, and potatoes. Cook 20 minutes.
4. Discard the bay leaves. Puree the soup. You can also leave a few chunks. It is up to you.
5. Now, combine the sour cream and flour in a bowl. Whisk and add a ½ cup of the soup. Whisk well. Now pour the mixture into the soup while stirring. Simmer for 5 to 10 minutes, until thickened—season with black pepper and salt to taste.
6. Cut kielbasa into circles. Add in the soup and add the horseradish. Stir.
7. Garnish with eggs, parsley, and dill. Serve and enjoy!

Note: You can also skip the blending and serve it with chunks.

POTATO PANCAKES

Prep Time: 20 Minutes
Cook Time: 30 Minutes
Serving: 4

Ingredients:

- 1kg potatoes
- Two eggs
- Four tablespoons of flour
- Four garlic cloves
- Four handfuls of marjoram
- Lard

- Pepper
- Salt

Directions:

1. Grate cooked potatoes in the bowl. Mix them with egg, flour, garlic, salt, pepper, and marjoram. Make dough.
2. Melt lard in a pan. Form pancakes and fry until golden.
3. Serve.

EGG AND BACON NAAN PIZZAS

Preparation time: 20 minutes

Cooking time: 21 minutes

Servings: 4

Ingredients

- Four pieces of naan bread (pizza style)
- 1 1/2 cups shredded mozzarella cheese
- 1/2 cup of grated cheddar cheese
- One tablespoon of unsalted butter
- Four strips of bacon
- One small tomato
- Four chives
- One avocado (large)
- Four eggs
- Salt
- Black pepper

Directions:

Ensure the oven is preheated to 400 °F. Line two large baking trays with parchment paper. Put aside. Line a large plate with paper towels. Put aside. Place the butter in a microwave-safe bowl. Microwave over 600W (350 F) for 20-30 seconds, or until melted. Place the naan pizza bread on one of the baking trays. Brush the surface of each naan pizza bread with melted butter using a tiny pastry brush.

Place the bacon strips on the other baking tray. Cut the tomato into cubes. Remove and discard the seeds. Put aside. Set aside the chives, which have been finely chopped. Cut the avocado in half. Remove and discard the pit. Use a spoon to peel the avocado pulp from the skin gently and lay it flat on the cutting board. Discard the peels. Cut the avocado crosswise into small ¼ slices.

Sprinkle an equal amount of mozzarella and cheddar cheese over each naan bread. Gently break an egg in the center of each naan pizza bread. Place both baking trays on the center rack of the oven. Bake for 15-17 minutes, until the cheese is golden, the egg white is cooked, and the bacon is brown and crisp. If the bacon is not fully cooked, remove the naan pizza bread and cook the bacon for 3-4 minutes more.

Remove the baking trays from the oven. Place the bacon on the paper towel-lined dinner plate to drain. Spread an equal amount of avocado slices and diced tomatoes on each pizza. Crumble the bacon with clean hands and sprinkle it evenly over the pizzas. Sprinkle the chopped chives over the pizzas. Season the top of the pizzas with salt and pepper. Cut into slices and serve.

EGG AND CHEESE CASSEROLE

Preparation time: 35 minutes

Cooking time: 48 minutes

Servings: 4

Ingredients

- 8 ounces of grated cheddar cheese
- 12 eggs
- 1/3 cup of whole milk
- One teaspoon of salt
- 1/4 teaspoon black pepper

Directions:

Make sur the oven is preheated to 400 °F. Spray a 9x13" baking dish with nonstick cooking spray. Beat the milk, eggs, salt, and black pepper in a large mixing bowl. Add grated cheese. Fold with a rubber spatula until the cheese is evenly distributed.

Pour the mixture into the prepared baking dish. Place the dish on the center rack of the preheated oven. Bake the casserole for 40-45 minutes, until golden brown on top and a toothpick in the center comes out clean. Remove the pan from the oven. Let the casserole cool for at least 12 minutes before serving. Cut the casserole into squares and place it on a plate with a large spoon.

POLISH FLUFFY WAFFLE

Preparation time: 5 minutes

Cooking time: 10 minutes

Servings: 4

Ingredients

- 1 1/2 cups of milk
- Six tablespoons unsalted butter, melted
- 2 cups all-purpose flour
- Four tablespoons granulated sugar
- Four teaspoons baking powder
- 1/2 teaspoon of salt
- Two eggs

- One teaspoon vanilla extract

Directions:

Preheat the waffle iron. Coat gently with nonstick cooking spray. In a large mixing basin, whisk the flour, sugar, baking powder, and salt. With the back of a spoon, make a well in the centre. Beat the two eggs in the milk until well combined. Pour the milk/egg mixture, butter, and vanilla into the well of the dry ingredients and beat until blended. The butter will be a bit lumpy, so don't over-mix. Spoon the batter into the preheated waffle iron and cook for 3 minutes or until the waffles are golden brown and crispy. Serve immediately or cool on a wire rack. —store leftovers in an airtight bag in the freezer.

POLISH AMERICAN GINGERBREAD PAN

Preparation time: 15 minutes

Cooking time: 15 minutes

Servings: 6

Ingredients

- One bell pepper, red, chopped
- One bell pepper, green, chopped
- One large onion, finely chopped
- 1 pound fresh Polish white sausage
- 2 cups of leftover kluski (or two large boiled potatoes, sliced)
- Six large eggs
- 1/2 cup cheese, grated
- Salt and pepper to taste

Directions:

First, preheat the oven to 400 °F. Remove the meat from the Polish sausage casings and place it in a large cast-iron skillet. After that add the onion and bell pepper and cook until the sausage is cooked through and the vegetables are tender. Add two tablespoons of butter.

Add kluski or potatoes and heat through. Add the eggs and stir over medium-high heat, constantly stirring until the eggs are cooked to your taste. Adjust herbs and sprinkle with cheese, cover the surface completely and place the skillet in the oven until the cheese has melted.

POLISH BABKA BREAD

Preparation time: 3 hours

Cooking time: 25 minutes

Servings: 2

Ingredients

- 1/2 cup unsalted butter, softened
- 1 cup of milk, scalded
- 4 cups of all-purpose flour
- 1/2 cup of sugar
- Four egg yolks
- One teaspoon of salt
- 1 cup of raisins, optional
- One packet of yeast
- 1/4 cup of lukewarm water
- One egg lightly beaten
- Two tablespoons of water

Directions:

Sprinkle the yeast over your lukewarm water, stir a little and then let it sit. To scald milk, pour the milk into a small saucepan and heat over high heat until the milk is almost boiling. Remove from heat and let cool. Meanwhile, combine butter and sugar in a mixing bowl with the paddle attachment. Mix salt to the egg yolks and mix well. Add to the butter and sugar mixture. Scrape the sides and blend to incorporate.

Mix in your active yeast mixture well. Alternately add flour and roasted milk in batches until incorporated. For around 7-8 minutes, or until the dough is smooth, combine all of the ingredients in a mixing bowl. If you're using raisins, mix them in at this point.

Take the dough from the paddle and place it in the mixing basin. Cover the bowl with a towel and place in a warm, dark place for 1 1/2 hours to rise. Then place a covered bowl inside with the door closed to let it rise. Another way is to turn on the oven for a moment until it reaches 100 F and then turn it off again.

Generously butter two large loaf pans. Remove the risen dough and knock it down. Cut the dough into two equal pieces. Place the dough in the two prepared loaf pans. Spread the dough with your fingers to evenly cover the bottom of your pan. Brush the tops of the doughs with the egg wash.

Cover loaf pan with a towel and place it in a dark, warm place to rise a second time. Let rise for about 52-57 minutes. Remove towel. Place the loaves in the preheated oven to 355 F. Bake for 26-32 minutes. Remove from the oven and let cool in the pan for 7 minutes. Then, take the loaves from the pan and place them on a cooling rack to cool. Otherwise, condensation will build upon the bottom of the loaves. Once the loaves have cooled enough, slice them and serve.

POLISH EASTER BREAKFAST RECIPE

Prep Time: 20 Minutes
Cook Time: 20 Minutes
Serving: 4

Ingredients:

- Olive oil, two tablespoons
- Eggs, four
- Horse radish root, one cup
- Smoked kielbasa, half cup

- Fresh kielbasa, one cup
- Chopped tomatoes, one cup
- Cured chopped ham, one cup
- Heavy cream, one cup
- Salt, to taste
- Black pepper, to taste

Directions:

1. Take a pan.
2. Add the chopped tomatoes to the pan.
3. Cook the tomatoes until they become soft.
4. Add the spices.
5. Add all kinds of meat into the pan.
6. Boil the eggs and then peel them.
7. Chop the boiled eggs well.
8. Add the eggs into the mixture.
9. Cook all the ingredients well, and then add the cream.
10. Cover the pan for five minutes.
11. Your dish is ready to be served.

POLISH EGG AND SAUSAGE STUFFED POTATOES RECIPE

Prep Time: 10 minutes
Cook Time: 20 minutes
Serving: 2

Ingredients:

- Smoked paprika, half teaspoon
- Hot sauce, one cup
- Ground sausage, two cups
- Minced garlic, two tablespoons
- Eggs, four
- Powdered cumin, one tablespoon
- Salt, to taste
- Black pepper, to taste
- Red onion, one cup
- Cilantro, half cup
- Olive oil, two tablespoons
- Small potatoes, four
- Chopped tomatoes, one cup
- Cheese, one cup

Directions:

1. Take a pan.
2. Add oil and onions into it.
3. Cook the onions until they are fragrant.

4. Add the garlic and mix it until its color changes.
5. Add in the chopped tomatoes.
6. Add the sausage.
7. Add in the spices, salt, and pepper.
8. Cook the mixture for fifteen minutes.
9. Add the eggs into the mixture.
10. Cook the mixture.
11. Clean the potatoes from inside.
12. Add the cooked mixture into the potatoes.
13. Add the shredded cheese on top.
14. Place the potatoes in a baking tray.
15. Bake the potatoes for ten minutes.
16. Garnish the cilantro on top.
17. Your dish is ready to be served.

POLISH OPEN-FACED SANDWICH

Prep Time: 30 minutes
Cook Time: 10 minutes
Serving: 4

Ingredients:

- Mayonnaise, two tablespoons
- Salad leaves, as required
- Heavy cream, half cup
- Lemon juice, three tablespoons
- Asino berries, as required
- Bread slices, as required
- Sugar, one tablespoon

Directions:

1. In a large bowl, combine the mayonnaise, heavy cream, lemon juice, and sugar until well combined.
2. Toast the bread slices.
3. Add the salad leaves to the bread slices.
4. On top of the slices, spread the mayonnaise, heavy cream, lemon juice, and sugar combination.
5. Add the casino berries on top.
6. The dish is ready to be served.

POLISH EGG & HAM ROLLUPS

Preparation Time: 30 minutes
Cooking Time: 20 mins Yield: 5

Ingredients:

- Six ham slices

- Six boiled eggs
- A drizzle of horseradish for each roll
- Two lemon wedges
- A drizzle of mayonnaise for each roll
- Five lettuce leaves
- Two large chopped tomatoes
- Two chopped chives
- Two sliced radishes

1. Directions:
   Boil eggs and then lengthwise cut them into quarters.
2. Take sliced boiled ham strips and spread them with a thin layer of horseradish and a thick layer of mayonnaise.
3. At the end of each strip, place the egg quarters and roll them up.
4. Take a narrow platter and align the roll-ups down the center.
5. Adorn a side with lettuce leaves and radishes, and the other side of platter with lemon wedges and tomato.
6. Finally, sprinkle chopped chives and serve.

POLISH BREAKFAST SANDWICH RECIPE

Prep time: 30 minutes
Cook Time: 15 minutes
Serving: 3

Ingredients:

- Cheese slices, as required
- Mayonnaise, half cup
- Eggs, six
- Vegetable oil, four teaspoons
- Onions, one
- Chopped garlic, one teaspoon
- Butter, two tablespoons
- Chopped tomatoes, half cup
- Kielbasa, one cup
- Salt, to taste

- Black pepper, to taste
- Bread slices, as required

Directions:

1. Take a large pan.
2. Add the onion and butter into it.
3. Cook the onions until it turns soft.
4. Add the chopped garlic into the pan along with the chopped tomatoes.
5. Cook the mixture and add the kielbasa into the pan.
6. Add salt and pepper into the pan.
7. Cook the mixture well and then dish it out.
8. Fry the eggs in the vegetable oil.
9. Toast the bread slices and spread the mayonnaise on each piece.
10. Place the kielbasa mixture and fried egg on the bread slices.
11. Add the cheese slice and top it with another slice of bread.
12. Your dish is ready to be served.

POLISH SAUSAGE AND HERB OMELET RECIPE

Prep Time: 30 minutes
Cook Time: 10 minutes
Serving: 4

Ingredients:

- Fresh herbs, a quarter cup
- Crushed red pepper, two teaspoons
- Chopped red onions, half cup
- Polish sausage slices, half cup
- Black pepper to taste
- Butter, as required
- Salt to taste
- Baby plum tomatoes, four
- Eggs, four
- Cilantro, half cup

Directions:

1. Take a large bowl.
2. Add the eggs, tomatoes, spices, sausage slices, onions, and herbs into the bowl.
3. Add the butter to a pan.
4. Heat the butter.
5. Do not incorporate the egg mixture into the pan.
6. Cook for a few minutes, or until the mixture is cooked on the bottom.
7. Flip the omelette.
8. Dish out the omelette and add the chopped cilantro on top.
9. The dish is ready to be served.

POLISH POTATO OVEN OMELET RECIPE

Prep Time: 30 minutes
Cook Time: 10 minutes
Serving: 4

Ingredients:

- Crushed red pepper, two teaspoons
- Chopped red onions, half cup
- Potato slices, half cup
- Black pepper to taste
- Butter, as required
- Salt to taste
- Baby plum tomatoes, four
- Eggs, four
- Cilantro, half cup
- Cheese, one cup

Directions:

1. Take a large bowl.
2. Add the eggs, tomatoes, spices, sausage slices, onions, and herbs into the bowl.
3. Grease a baking dish with butter.
4. Add the egg mixture into the baking dish and add the cheese on top.
5. Bake the omelette for ten to fifteen minutes.
6. Dish out the omelette and add the chopped cilantro on top.
7. The dish is ready to be served.

POLISH STUFFED EGGS RECIPE

Prep Time: 10 minutes
Cook Time: 20 minutes
Serving: 2

Ingredients:

- Smoked paprika, half teaspoon
- Hot sauce, one cup
- Ground sausage, two cups
- Minced garlic, two tablespoons
- Eggs, four
- Powdered cumin, one tablespoon
- Salt, to taste
- Black pepper, to taste
- Red onion, one cup
- Cilantro, half cup
- Olive oil, two tablespoons
- Chopped tomatoes, one cup

- Cheese, one cup

Directions:

1. Take a pan.
2. Add oil and onions into it.
3. Cook the onions until they are fragrant.
4. Add the garlic and mix it until its color changes.
5. Add in the chopped tomatoes.
6. Add the sausage.
7. Add in the spices, salt, and pepper.
8. Cook the mixture for fifteen minutes.
9. Boil the eggs and peel them.
10. Remove the egg yolk and crush it.
11. Add the egg yolk mixture into the sausage mixture.
12. Mix both the things well and fill the boiled eggs with the mixture.
13. Add the shredded cheese on top.
14. Place the eggs in a baking tray.
15. Bake the eggs for ten minutes.
16. Garnish the cilantro on top.
17. Your dish is ready to be served.

COTTAGE CHEESE AND HERBS

Prep Time: 10 minutes
Cook Time: 20 minutes
Serving: 2

Ingredients:

- ½ lb. Cottage cheese, Polish style
- 2 tbsp. Oil
- 5 tbsp. Herbs Mix (Chives, parsley, basil, dill, and mint)
- 1 tsp. Ground black pepper
- 5 oz. Yogurt
- Cherry Tomatoes
- Rye Bread

Directions:

1. In a bowl, add cottage cheese. Mash with a fork.
2. Add the remaining ingredients. Mix well.
3. Serve with cherry tomatoes and rye bread and enjoy!

HOMEMADE KOLACHE

Preparation time: 4 hours

Cooking time: 15 minutes

Servings: 3

Ingredients

- Two eggs
- 1/2 cup plus 1/4 cup melted butter
- One packet of yeast
- 1 cup of warm milk
- 1/4 cup sugar
- 3 cups of flour
- One teaspoon of salt
- Fillings of your choice

Directions:

Stir yeast, warm milk, sugar, and 1 cup flour in a large mixing basin. Mix well, cover, and let it rise until doubled in size for at least 35 minutes. Mix egg, 1/2 cup of melted butter, and salt in a separate bowl. Add to yeast mixture. Mix in 2 ½ cups of flour or a little more. The dough should be soft and moist. Knead for 11 minutes. Place in a greased bowl and let rise for at least 70 minutes or until doubled.

Knock down the dough and pull-out pieces, about 3-inch in size. Place them on a greased baking sheet and flatten them to about 5 inches wide. Smaller for the jam-covered, larger for the ones filled). Brush with melted butter and place the filling in the center.

Pull up the sides to cover the filling and squeeze together to seal. Turnover, so the sealed side is at the bottom. Let rise for 30 minutes. For jam, let Kolaches rise for 30 minutes, then make holes in the top and fill with spoons of jam. Bake for 13-15 minutes at 375°F in a preheated oven. When they come out of the oven, brush them with extra melted butter.

POLISH APPLE PANCAKES

Preparation time: 75 minutes

Cooking time: 30 minutes

Servings: 6

- Ingredients
- Two eggs, beaten
- One tablespoon of salted butter, melted and cooled slightly
- 2½ cups unbleached all-purpose flour
- One tablespoon of sugar
- Two teaspoons active dry yeast
- 1/4 teaspoon of salt
- 1½ cup lukewarm milk
- Two large apples
- ½ cup rapeseed oil (for frying)
- Icing sugar

Directions:

Combine the sugar, flour, yeast, and salt in a bowl. Add the melted butter, milk, and eggs. Mix until the mixture is moist and thick. Cover the batter and place it in a warm, draft-free place to rise for 85 minutes—Peel, core, and dice the apples towards the end of the rising time. Once the dough has risen, stir in the diced apples.

Add two tablespoons of oil to cover the bottom of a 12-inch sauté pan. Heat the oil over medium heat. Spoon the butter into the hot pan and spread it as thinly as possible with the thick apple pieces in between. Bake the pancakes for 3 minutes until the bottom is golden brown. Turn the pancakes over and cook on the other side for 2-3 minutes, until golden brown; then remove the pancakes from the pan and place them on a paper-lined plate.

Repeat the process with the remaining dough, adding more oil as necessary. While the remainder of the pancakes are cooking, keep the completed ones warm. In general, pancakes are best crispy and fresh from the pan, so try to serve them straight. Sprinkle with icing sugar before serving.

BAKED POLISH PACZKI

Preparation time: 4 hours

Cooking time: 10 minutes

Servings: 24

Ingredients

- Two eggs
- Four egg yolks
- Two tablespoons of brandy
- 1½ cup lukewarm milk
- 1 ½ tablespoon of active dry yeast
- 1/3 cup unsalted butter, softened
- ¼ cup of sugar
- One teaspoon of salt
- 6 cups unbleached all-purpose flour
- 1 cup smooth jam, pastry cream, or lemon curd
- 1 cup icing sugar or granulated sugar

Directions:

Add the warm milk to a small bowl. Sprinkle the yeast over the milk and let it rest for 5 minutes so that the yeast becomes soft and foamy. Cream the sugar and butter in an electric mixer equipped with a paddle attachment until pale and creamy. Add the brandy, eggs, yolks, and salt. Beat until combined and smooth. On low speed, add one-third of the milk mixture, alternating with flour, until 5 cups flour has been added. When the dough comes together, switch from the paddle attachment to the dough hooks. On medium speed, mix until the mixture comes together, adding additional flour as needed. The dough should be soft and sticky without becoming runny.

Increase the speed of the mixer to medium and knead the dough for 6-7 minutes until smooth and shiny. Pull the dough from the dough hooks and wrap it in a moist tea towel in the bowl. Allow the dough to rise for 90 min in a warm, draft-free environment, or until doubled in size.

Place it on a well-floured work surface when the dough has risen and knock it down. Roll out the dough to ½ inch thickness. Use 3-inch circular cookie cutter to cut circles from the dough. Roll again and cut, if necessary, until all dough is cut. Place the rounds on a baking tray lined with parchment paper. Cover the circles lightly with your damp kitchen towel and let them rise for about 45 minutes or until puffy and nearly doubled.

By the end of the rising time, heat your oven to 375 F and bake the doughnuts for 7-10 minutes in the preheated oven until a toothpick in the center of one of the doughnuts comes out clean. Let the doughnuts cool on the baking tray for 2-3 minutes before placing them on a wire rack. If you are filling your paczki, do this after 10 minutes or once they are cool enough to handle. Fill it with the desired jam or custard filling. Put the tip of the pastry bag into the center of the paczki as far as possible. Gently squeeze the pastry bag while slowly pulling the tip out of the doughnut. You will feel the paczki gain weight as you fill them with about two tablespoons of the filling.

If you're going to sugar your doughnuts with granulated sugar, roll them in it while they're still warm so the sugar sticks. If you're using powdered sugar to sugar your doughnuts, wait for them to cool completely before rolling them in powdered sugar.

SAUSAGE WITH VEGETABLES

Preparation time: 12 minutes

Cooking time: 30 minutes

Servings: 4

Ingredients:

- 1/2 medium onion, chopped
- 1/2 medium green pepper, seeded, chopped
- 1 1/2 cups sliced mushrooms
- Two medium Yukon Gold potatoes, peeled, cut into 1/2-inch cubes
- Two tablespoons of unsalted butter
- 6 ounces smoked sausage, sliced 1/4-inch thick
- 1/4 cup of whole milk
- Six eggs
- Salt and pepper

Directions:

Place the potatoes and two teaspoons salt in a large, deep saucepan and add enough water to cover the potatoes 1-inch above them. Rise to a boil over high heat and simmer for 7-10 minutes or until potatoes are just tender. Drain and wipe the skillet away.

Melt butter in the same skillet over 325 F. Add sausage pieces. Cook, occasionally stirring until browned on both sides, about 4 minutes. Move to a bowl with a slotted spoon. Add vegetables to the pan and season with salt and pepper. Cook on medium to high heat, stirring occasionally for 8-9 minutes or until mushrooms are browned and tender vegetables.

Beat the eggs with milk in a medium bowl—season with salt and pepper. Add sausage and potatoes to vegetables in a skillet and stir to combine. Pour in the egg mixture and cook, constantly stirring for 1-2 minutes or until the eggs are set but still creamy. Serve immediately.

MUSHROOM SOUP

Preparation time: 15 minutes

Cooking time: 15 minutes

Servings: 6

Ingredients:

- Three carrots
- Two parsnips
- 1/2 celery root
- One package of dried mushrooms
- One container of fresh mushrooms
- One-piece beef with round bone
- One large onion
- Four large potatoes

Directions:

1. Peel and wash all your vegetables. Dice all vegetables.
2. Use the boiling water to rehydrate the dried mushrooms. Allow them to soak for at least a half-hour.
3. Put all of your veggies, meat, and salt and pepper to taste in a big saucepan filled with water. Cook until the water begins to boil, then reduce the heat to low.
4. Fry the fresh mushrooms in a frying pan until golden brown, then add them to the soup. Fry the onions and add them to the soup.
5. Put the soaked dried mushrooms, along with the water they soaked in, into the soup. Allow it to simmer for an hour on low heat.
6. At the very end, I extract the flesh off the bone. Return the meat to the broth, cut into tiny pieces.
7. Sprinkle with fresh herbs before serving.

PICKLE SOUP

Preparation time: 15 minutes

Cooking time: 25 minutes

Servings: 6

Ingredients:

- 8 cups chicken or vegetable stock
- 1 pound peeled and quartered potatoes
- Two large peeled and diced carrots
- One large peeled and diced parsnip
- One rib diced celery
- Six shredded dill pickles
- 1 cup sour cream
- Chopped fresh dill

Directions:

1. Heat the stock to a boil in a large saucepan. Toss in the potatoes, carrots, parsnip, and celery. Transfer to a boil, then reduce to a low heat and cook until the veggies are soft.
2. Mix in the pickles and any accumulated juices.
3. In a small heatproof dish, temper the sour cream by continually whisking in a few ladles of boiling soup.
4. Transfer the tempered sour cream to the soup and heat until it begins to simmer, but not boil, otherwise the sour cream will break.
5. Now serve hot in warmed bowls with chopped fresh dill and caraway-seed rye bread pieces.

POTATO SOUP

Preparation time: 15 minutes

Cooking time: 35 minutes

Servings: 6

Ingredients:

- 1 1/2 cup sliced potatoes
- 1 cup of sliced beets
- One and a half cups of chopped onion
- 3 cups of chopped red cabbage
- 1/4 teaspoon of fresh dill
- Two tablespoons of butter
- One teaspoon of caraway seed
- One chopped celery stalk
- One large sliced carrot
- One tablespoon of cider vinegar

- One tablespoon of honey
- 1 cup of tomato puree
- Two teaspoons of salt
- Black pepper to taste

Directions:

1. Boil potatoes and beets until tender.
2. Remove potatoes and beets. Reserve stock.
3. Meanwhile, melt butter in a large saucepan.
4. Stir in onion, caraway seeds, and salt. Fry until the onion turns to gold. Stir in celery, carrot, and cabbage.
5. Mix in the reserved stock and cook for about 10 minutes.
6. Add potatoes, beets, and tomato puree.
7. Reduce heat to medium and boil for at least 30 minutes.
8. Serve the soup topped with sour cream and dill.

MEDIEVAL HUNTING SOUP

Preparation time: 10 minutes

Cooking time: 40 minutes

Servings: 4

Ingredients

- Two thick slices of smoked bacon
- 1 1/2 cups sliced mushrooms
- pound cubed beef stew meat
- One teaspoon dried marjoram
- Two carrots
- 1/4 cup all-purpose flour
- Three cloves garlic
- 1 pound kielbasa sausage
- One onion
- 4 cups green cabbage, shredded
- 1 (16 ounces) jar sauerkraut
- 1/8 teaspoon caraway seed
- One bay leaf
- One teaspoon dried basil
- 1 cup diced tomatoes
- One tablespoon sweet paprika
- 1/4 cup vinegar
- 1/8 teaspoon black pepper
- One dash Worcestershire sauce
- One pinch of cayenne pepper
- 1/2-ounce dried mushrooms
- 1/4 teaspoon salt
- One dash bottled hot pepper sauce

- 5 cups beef stock
- Two tablespoons tomato paste

Directions

1. Make sure the oven is preheated to 400 °F.
2. In a pot, fry the bacon and sausage for about 5 minutes and add to a casserole dish.
3. Toss the beef meat into flour and add the remaining oil left from the bacon to the pot.
4. Add the vegetables and mushrooms and cook for about 10 minutes.
5. Add the pot's vinegar, basil, salt, bay leaf, marjoram, caraway seeds, pepper, and cayenne pepper.
6. Toss for just 5 minutes and add the diced tomatoes, hot pepper sauce, beef stock, Worcestershire sauce, and tomato paste.
7. Cook until it boils and take off the heat.
8. Pour into the casserole dish and bake in the oven for about 2 hours.

BLACK SOUP

Preparation time: 10 minutes

Cooking time: 15 minutes

Servings: 5

Ingredients:

- One whole duck
- 4 cups of duck blood
- 8 cups of water
- Two whole garlic cloves
- 500g pitted prunes
- 1/2 cup of raisins
- One apple
- One stalk of celery
- Two tablespoons of flour
- One tablespoon of sugar
- One chopped sprig of parsley
- 1 cup of cooking cream
- Five whole allspice pieces
- One tablespoon of lemon juice
- Salt

Directions:

1. Boil the whole duck, celery, parsley, allspice, and garlic cloves for one and half hours. You can put the vegetable and spices in a cloth bag.
2. Remove vegetables and duck. Discard bones. Cut meat and return it to the broth.
3. Mix in sliced prunes, raisins, and chopped apples.
4. Simmer for 30 minutes.

5. Meanwhile, beat flour, cream, and sugar in a medium bowl.
6. Add duck blood. Mix it well.
7. Add 1/2 of hot soup, stop, and mix it well again.
8. Pour the mixture into the pot. Stirring in constantly and boiling it for a while.
9. Serve.

TRIPE SOUP

Preparation time: 10 minutes

Cooking time: 20 minutes

Servings: 6

Ingredients:

- 500g beef tripes
- 500g pork stomachs
- Two marrowbones
- 300g root vegetables
- Four garlic cloves
- One tablespoon of flour
- One tablespoon of sweet paprika
- Marjoram
- Lard
- Black pepper
- Pinch of salt

Directions:

1. Boil tripes and stomach for 20 minutes with marrowbones in saltwater.
2. Meanwhile, fry diced vegetables in lard.
3. Remove tripes, stomachs, and marrowbones.
4. Slice tripes and stomachs into strips and put them back.
5. Add vegetable, garlic, salt, and pepper.
6. Make a roux from sweet paprika and flour.
7. Add to the broth.
8. Serve with marjoram.

POLISH KRAUT SOUP

Preparation time: 15 minutes

Cooking time: 30 minutes

Servings: 6

Ingredients:

- 14 oz. sauerkraut
- One lb. kielbasa

- 5 cups water
- 8-10 chicken bouillon cubes
- ½ tsp. white pepper
- Four celery stalks
- Three carrots
- ½ yellow onion
- One russet potato

Directions:

1. Boil water and meanwhile chop vegetables and diced kielbasa Squeeze some juice from your sauerkraut.
2. Add spices, bouillon, vegetables except for potatoes, kielbasa, and sauerkraut when the water boils. Boil again for almost 3 minutes and simmer.
3. Finally, add the potatoes and simmer again for 20 more minutes.

SPLIT PEA AND SAUSAGE SOUP

Prep Time: 20 minutes
Cook Time: 40 minutes
Serving: 4

Ingredients:

- 12 oz. split dried peas
- 2 14-oz. cans beef broth
- 16 oz. kielbasa sausage
- One onion
- 1 cup chopped carrots
- One bay leaf
- Salt and black pepper to taste

Directions:

1. Cut kielbasa sausage into cubes. Reserve ¼ of the sausage and place it along with beef broth (½ can) in the blender.
2. In the soup pot, pour half the beef broth cans and allow it to boil. Meanwhile, add onion diced and cubes of sausage. Then, add the bay leaf and a pinch of pepper and salt. Simmer for half an hour.
3. Put sliced carrots in it. Continue to simmer for ten more minutes.
4. Wash split peas and add them to the simmering pot. Add salt and pepper according to your taste and simmer.
5. Serve well.

PEA SOUP

Preparation time: 10 minutes

Cooking time: 35 minutes

Servings: 3

Ingredients:

- 1.5l beef broth
- 500g pea
- Two slices of ham
- Two tablespoons of flour
- Two tablespoons of butter
- One tablespoon of sweet paprika
- Two tablespoons of marjoram
- Two garlic cloves
- Black pepper
- Pinch of salt

Directions:

1. Boil pea in broth for 30 minutes.
2. Meanwhile, fry ham and garlic in butter.
3. Blend the pea with a hand blender.
4. Add flour and make the roux. Add sweet paprika.
5. Add roux to the broth. Add pepper, salt, marjoram and cook for 20 minutes.
6. Serve with fresh bread.

COLD BORSHCH

Preparation time: 15 minutes

Cooking time: 45 minutes

Servings: 3

Ingredients:

- Five young, tender beets, with tops
- Two cucumbers, peeled and grated
- Six radishes, grated
- Two green onions, chopped
- 4 cups plain yogurt
- 4 cups buttermilk
- 1 cup sour cream
- Three hardboiled eggs, quartered
- Three tablespoons dill, chopped
- 1/2 teaspoon salt
- Salt and pepper, to taste

Directions:

1. Remove and dice the stems up to the leaves of the beets.
2. In a large soup saucepan, combine the chopped stems.
3. Add the remaining beetroots to the pan after peeling and grating them. Add the water to cover the beets and season with salt.
4. Simmer for 15 minutes, or until the vegetables are soft.
5. Allow the beet mixture to cool.

6. Combine the cucumbers, radishes, dill, green onions, yogurt, kefir, and sour cream in a mixing bowl.
7. Season with salt and pepper to taste.
8. Chill and serve with a hardboiled egg on top.

CHEESY POTATO SOUP

Preparation time: 15 minutes

Cooking time: 28 minutes

Servings: 4

Ingredients:

- 6 cups water
- Eight oz. cream cheese
- 3 Yukon gold potatoes
- ½ cup crumbled bacon
- 1 cup cheddar cheese

Directions:

1. Firstly, peel and cube potatoes. Then, boil them in water till they turn soft.
2. Season with salt and pepper.
3. Reduce heat to medium.
4. Cut small pieces of cream cheese and add them to the potatoes in equal parts.
5. Cook and heat until cream cheese melts and blends.
6. Finally, add bacon, shredded cheese and serve.

POLISH BEET SOUP

Prep Time: 30 minutes
Cook Time: 20 minutes
Serving: 4

Ingredients:

- Olive oil, two tablespoons
- Chopped carrots, one cup
- Lime juice, half cup
- Chopped celery, one cup
- Chopped tomatoes, one cup
- Mix spice powder, one teaspoon
- Onion, one cup
- Chopped fresh parsley, as required
- Smoked paprika, half teaspoon
- Bay leaf, one
- Sliced beetroot, one cup
- Salt, to taste
- Black pepper, to taste
- Vegetable broth, two cups

Directions:

1. Take a frying pan.
2. Put the oil and onions in a pan.
3. Cook until the onions are tender and aromatic.
4. Add the tomatoes into it.
5. Add the spices.
6. When the tomatoes are done, add the sliced beets, celery, carrots, and stock into it.
7. Let the soup cook for ten to fifteen minutes straight.
8. Add parsley on top.
9. Your dish is ready to be served.

HEARTY POLISH POTATO AND CHEESE SOUP

Prep Time: 20 minutes
Cook Time: 40 minutes
Serving: 4

Ingredients:

- 2 tbsp. butter
- 1 ½ cups of onion, chopped
- 3 tbsp. all-purpose flour
- 4 cups of whole milk
- Three potatoes, cut into small cubes
- ¼ tsp. black pepper

- 2 cups of Cheddar cheese, shredded
- 8 ounces of cooked Polish sausage, cut into thin slices
- Dash of salt

Directions:

1. Add the butter into a 4-quart saucepan placed over medium heat. Once the butter begins to sizzle, add in the chopped onions. Cook for almost 4 to 5 minutes or until soft.
2. Add in the flour and stir to coat—Cook for an additional minute.
3. Then add the whole milk, potato cubes, and black pepper. Stir to mix and continue to cook for 3 to 5 minutes or until the mixture reaches a boil.
4. Reduce the heat to low and cover. Cook over low heat for 22 to 28 minutes or until the potatoes are tender.
5. Add in the shredded Cheddar cheese and cooked Polish sausage. Continue to cook for 3 to 4 minutes or until the shredded cheese is melted.
6. Remove from the heat and season with a touch of salt. Serve while hot.

POLISH DILL PICKLE SOUP

Preparation and Cooking Time: 65 minutes

Serving: 7
Ingredients:

- One lb. beef neck bones
- 1 cup mixed vegetables
- 2 cups diced dill pickles
- 2 quarts water
- 2 cups diced potatoes
- 3 tbsps. all-purpose flour
- 1 cup milk
- salt to taste

Directions:

1. Put the pickles, vegetables, and neck bones in a big pot. Add in water and cook for 45 minutes on medium heat.
2. Put potatoes and cook for about 20 minutes until tender.
3. Take off the neck bones, then turn up the heat to medium-high. Mix the milk and flour in a small bowl, then slowly stir it into the soup. Keep on mixing until the mixture boils. Put salt to season.

CABBAGE SOUP

Preparation time: 10 minutes

Cooking time: 35 minutes

Servings: 4

Ingredients:

- 400g potatoes
- 400g sauerkraut

- 200g sausage
- One onion
- One garlic clove
- One tablespoon sweet paprika
- Two tablespoons lad
- 100g sour cream
- One tablespoon flour
- Pinch of salt
- Black pepper
- Crushed cumin

Directions:

1. Boil diced potatoes with salt and cumin for 20 minutes.
2. Fry diced onion in lard in a pan.
3. Add sauerkraut pour 1 liter water and add paprika.
4. Boil for 10 minutes.
5. Meanwhile, make the roux by frying flour with sour cream.
6. Add sauerkraut roux, cut sausage to the potatoes, and cook for 10 minutes.
7. Serve with fresh bread.

BARLEY SOUP

Preparation time: 10 minutes

Cooking time: 35 minutes

Servings: 4

Ingredients:

- 500g dried porcini mushrooms
- 13 cups stock
- Two small carrots
- Two small turnips
- Two small onions
- Two medium potatoes
- Two stalks celery and leaves
- 3/4 cup pearl barley
- Sour cream

Directions:

1. Soak the cepes in a small amount of water for 15 minutes, or until they soften.
2. In a food processor, finely chop all of the veggies in two batches and place them in a pan with the barley and broth.
3. In a food processor, chop the softened mushrooms and add them to the saucepan.
4. Rise to a boil, then skim the scum and season with salt and pepper to taste. Simmer for 1 hour.
5. The barley will thicken the soup.
6. Serve with sour cream.

BROTH WITH NOODLES

Preparation time: 10 minutes

Cooking time: 20 minutes

Servings: 4

Ingredients:

- 1/2 chicken with bones
- 500g beef with bones
- Two carrots
- One parsley root
- One celery
- 1/2 leek
- Two dried mushrooms
- One onion
- One teaspoon of black peppercorns
- Two dried bay leaves

Directions:

1. Boil meat in 2 liters of water for 1 hour.
2. Add carrot, parsley, celery, leek, mushrooms, and onion. Don't forget to add salt, peppercorns, and bay leaves.
3. Boil for an additional hour.
4. Remove meat and vegetable. Slice vegetables and return them.
5. Serve with noodles.

SORREL SOUP

Preparation time: 10 minutes

Cooking time: 15 minutes

Servings: 3

Ingredients:

- 200g fresh sorrel, washed, stemmed as for spinach, and chopped
- 6 cups cold water
- One large peeled and sliced carrot
- One bunch of fresh parsley
- One bay leaf
- Three peeled and cubed medium potatoes
- One chicken or vegetable bouillon cube
- One tablespoon butter
- 1 cup sour cream
- One tablespoon all-purpose flour
- Chopped fresh dill or parsley
- Two hard-cooked eggs cut into quarters
- Salt and pepper to taste

Directions:

1. Place 6 cups of cold water, carrots, and parsley in a large saucepan. Heat the water to a boil, then add the bay leaf, potatoes, and bouillon cube. Bring back to a boil, then lower to a low heat and continue to cook until the veggies are soft.
2. Now melt butter in a large pan and sauté sorrel for 10 minutes. Bring the soup to a boil in the meantime. Reduce the heat. Take out the bay leaf.
3. Fork-blend sour cream and flour in a heatproof basin or measuring cup, then temper with a few spoonful of boiling soup, whisking continually until smooth.
4. Pour in the tempered sour cream-flour mixture, stir well, and cook until thickened and just under the boiling point. Season to taste.
5. To serve, spoon soup into warmed bowls and top with chopped dill or parsley and egg quarters.

TOMATO SOUP

Preparation time: 15 minutes

Cooking time: 45 minutes

Servings: 4

Ingredients:

- 1l vegetable broth
- 400g peeled tomatoes
- One can of tomato sauce
- Four tablespoons of olive oil
- One onion
- Four garlic cloves
- Two bay leaf
- Three allspice
- One tablespoon of sugar
- Black pepper

- Pinch of salt
- Basil
- Cooked pasta

Directions:

1. Fry diced onion in oil.
2. Add garlic. Add peeled tomatoes (whole).
3. Pour vegetable broth and add a bay leaf with allspice (best in teabag).
4. Boil for 10 minutes.
5. Remove all spices and blend the soup.
6. Add tomato sauce and sugar.
7. Serve with basil and cooked rice.

RYE SOUP

Preparation time: 15 minutes

Cooking time: 30 minutes

Servings: 3

Ingredients:

- Kwas:
- 75g wholemeal rye flour
- 600ml boiled, cooled water
- 1/4 garlic clove

Soup:

- 1 1/4 l vegetable stock
- 100g bacon
- 100g onions
- One can mushroom
- 400ml was
- 300ml sour cream
- Five medium potatoes, cooked and diced
- 100g smoked sausage, diced

Directions:

1. A non-aluminum container, such as an earthenware jar, can be rinsed with hot water to remove any residue.
2. Fill the jar halfway with flour and mix it into a liquid paste with a little water. Leave for several minutes for the mixture to settle before adding the remaining warm water.
3. Add the garlic, chopped.
4. Cover the jar with muslin or punctured cling film and keep it in a warm area to ferment for 4 to 5 days.
5. Use as needed after straining.
6. If kept in a sealed jar, it will remain for a few weeks. Warm the stock.

7. Chop the bacon and onion and add them to the stock.
8. Cook for 10 minutes.
9. Season with salt and pepper and add the mushrooms, kvass, cream, and garlic.
10. Allow to boil for 20 minutes before adding the potatoes and meat.
11. Bring water to a boil.
12. Serve in hollowed bread.

STUFFED CABBAGE

Preparation time: 30min
Cooking time: 1h

Servings: 9

Ingredients:

- One whole Cabbage head
- 1 Onion, chopped
- ½ lb. Ground Pork
- 1 lb. Ground Beef
- 1 ½ cup cooked Rice
- 1 tsp. Garlic, chopped
- 1 tsp. Salt
- ¼ tsp. Black pepper
- 1 cup of Beef Stock
- Optional: Sour cream for garnish
- Oil

Directions:

1. Remove the core from the Cabbage.
2. Fill a pot with water, season with salt, and place the cabbage. Cook for 3 minutes covered. You need about 18 leaves.
3. Let the cabbage cool. Once cooled, cut the steam from the leaves but don't cut the whole stem, just the thick center.
4. Chop the cabbage that you won't use and layer it in a casserole dish.

5. Turn on medium-high heat and place a skillet. Add the onion and drizzle with oil. Cook for 5 minutes. Set aside to cool.
6. In a bowl, combine the pork and beef meat and add black pepper, salt, garlic, and rice. Mix well until combined.
7. Now add ½ cup meat mixture to each leaf.
8. Flip the left and the right side.
9. Now roll the lead and transfer it into the casserole dish. Repeat the process with all cabbage leaves. Season each layer with salt and black pepper to taste.
10. Heat the oven, 350F. Pour 1 cup of beef stock. Cover the dish and cook for about 1 hour.
11. Serve with the juices from the casserole dish and sour cream.
12. Enjoy!

BEEF ROULADE

Preparation time: 30min
Cooking time: 1h

Servings: 4

Ingredients:

- Eight steaks for a sandwich, pounded into 1/8-inch-thick steak (trimmed)
- 2-3 dill pickles, sliced into strips
- 4 oz. Ham, strips
- 2-3 green onions, cut into strips
- 4 tbsp. Oil
- 2 tbsp. Flour
- 1 cup of beef stock
- 4 tbsp. White Wine
- 1 tbsp. Tomato Paste
- 1 tsp. Of Salt
- ½ tsp. Black pepper
- Sour Cream for garnish
- Chopped Parsley for garnish

Directions:

1. Spread mustard on the steaks. Divide the onion, ham, and pickles evenly between the steaks. Fold the sides, then roll. Secure using a toothpick.
2. Add oil to a Dutch oven and heat over medium-high heat. Brown the rolls and set them aside.
3. In the same pan, add the flour and cook until lightly browned. Add the tomato paste, wine, and stock—season with black pepper and salt. Reduce the heat to low and continue to cook for 1 minute.
4. Retune the rolls and spoon some sauce over them. Cover. Cook 45min-1h on low. Add more liquid if needed.
5. Once cooked, transfer them to a serving dish. Remove toothpicks—ladle sauce over the rolls.
6. Serve with parsley and sour cream. Serve with rice or mashed potatoes as a side dish.
7. Enjoy!

AUTHENTIC POLISH PICKLE SOUP

Preparation time: 10 minutes

Cooking time: 50 minutes

Servings: 6

Ingredients:

- Two chicken leg quarters, skin removed
- 1/2 small head green cabbage, chopped
- 5 cups water, or as needed to cover
- Two carrots, peeled and sliced
- Two stalks celery, sliced
- One onion, sliced
- Two bay leaves
- 3 tbsps. chopped fresh parsley
- One clove garlic, minced
- One pinch ground thyme
- One pinch dried marjoram
- salt and ground black pepper to taste
- Four small dill pickles, thinly sliced
- 1 tbsp. all-purpose flour
- 1/4 cup sour cream

Directions:

1. Add the chicken legs into the big pot and cover with the water. Put in the black pepper, salt, marjoram, thyme, garlic, parsley, bay leaves, onion, celery, carrots, and cabbage.
2. Keep the pot covered and simmer on medium heat—Cook for roughly 60 minutes. Move 1 cup of the vegetable and chicken broth to the saucepan. Heat the pickles and broth on medium-low for roughly 15 minutes. Bring the pickle broth back to the big pot.
3. In the bowl, combine the sour cream and flour. Mix to the soup; boil roughly 5 minutes or till becoming thick. Serve right away.

BAKED CHICKEN REUBEN

Preparation time: 10 minutes

Cooking time: 50 minutes

Servings: 6

Ingredients:

- Six skinless, boneless chicken breast halves
- 1/4 tsp. salt
- 1/8 tsp. ground black pepper
- 1 (16 oz.) can sauerkraut, drained and pressed

- 4 slices Swiss cheese
- 1 1/4 cups thousand islands salad dressing
- 1 tbsp. chopped fresh parsley

Directions:

1. Set an oven to preheat at 165°C (325°F).
2. In a 9x13 inch lightly greased baking dish, place in the chicken. Sprinkle pepper and salt to season. Top the chicken with sauerkraut and put cheese slices on top. Pour the dressing all over the cover the dish with aluminum foil.
3. Bake in the preheated oven until the chicken is cooked through (juices run clear and can easily be pricked with a fork) or for 90 minutes. Sprinkle chopped parsley on top, then serve.

BASIC BABKA

Preparation time: 10 minutes

Cooking time: 50 minutes

Servings: 6

Ingredients: For Dough:

- 1/2 cup white sugar
- 1/4 cup butter
- 1 tsp. salt
- 1 cup hot milk (185 degrees F (85 degrees C))
- 2 (.25 oz.) packages active dry yeast
- Two eggs
- 1/4 cup warm water (110 degrees F (43 degrees C))
- 4 1/2 cups all-purpose flour

For Walnut Filling:

- Three eggs
- 1 cup packed light brown sugar
- 1/3 cup butter, melted
- 1 1/2 tsp. ground cinnamon
- 1 tsp. vanilla extract
- 4 cups walnuts, chopped
- 2 tbsps. butter, melted

Directions:

1. In a small bowl, mix salt, 1/4 cup of butter, and white sugar into the hot milk till butter is melted and the mixture becomes lukewarm. Scatter the yeast over warm water in the work bowl of a stand mixer attached with the paddle; mix to dissolve.
2. Into yeast mixture, mix the milk mixture. Put in 2 1/2 cups flour and two eggs; whip on high speed till blended. Put in leftover 2 cups flour, a half cup at a time, using the mixer on low.

3. Put the dough in a lightly oiled big bowl, flipping dough to coat the surface. Change into dough hook; combine for 5 minutes till dough pulls away from bowl sides. Put on a towel to cover and rise in a warm area for an hour till doubled.
4. Meanwhile, make the walnut filling. In a big bowl, lightly whip three eggs: mix vanilla extract, cinnamon, 1/3 cup melted butter, and brown sugar. Fold in the walnuts.
5. Punch down dough. Transfer dough to a big, lightly floured area, put a bowl to cover and allow to sit for 10 minutes. Line parchment paper on three loaf pans, 9x5 inches in size, keeping a 2-inch overhang on long sides.
6. Split the dough into three portions; on a lightly floured area, unroll every part into a square, 12 inches in size. Onto every dough square, scoop 1/3 of walnut filling, and spread, leaving a half-inch border. Tightly roll every square up, jelly-roll style—press seams and ends to enclose. Roll cylinder forward and backward with your palms till evenly round.
7. To make two striped strands, halve a cylinder lengthwise using a dough scraper or sharp knife. Working quickly, loosely twist the strands together, cut sides out, creating 2 to 3 wide horizontal twists. Fit into a prepped pan, tapping back any loose filling and tucking ends beneath, if necessary. It may seem a mess at this time, yet it gets out wonderful.
8. Do the same with the rest of the pans and cylinders. Put a towel over pans to cover and allow to rise in a warm area for an hour till doubled in size. Loaves must not increase over the pan's top edges.
9. Preheat an oven to 175°C or 350°F. Brush leftover 2 tbsps. Of melted butter on top of the loaf.
10. Let loaves bake for 35 to 45 minutes till nicely browned, puffed, and a thermometer pricked in centers reads 93°C or 200°F. Tent with foil in case surfaces brown before loaves are finished. Cool for 10 minutes in pans, then lift the pans using the parchment and turn onto the wire rack.
11. Cool fully for an hour. Glaze if wished, then cut crosswise and serve.

POLISH HUNTER'S STEW

Preparation Time: 10 minutes
Cooking Time: 40 minutes
Serving: 2

Ingredients:

- Beef broth, two cups
- Cumin powder, one teaspoon
- Onion, one cup

- Lemon juice, half cup
- Hunter beef, half pound
- Smoked paprika, half teaspoon
- Minced garlic, two tablespoons
- Cilantro, half cup
- Olive oil, two tablespoons
- Water, two cups
- Heavy cream, one cup

Directions:

1. Take a pan.
2. Add in the oil and onions.
3. Cook the onions until they become soft and fragrant.
4. Add in the chopped garlic and ginger.
5. Cook the mixture and add the hunter beef into it.
6. Add the spices and water.
7. Boil the stew and add the cream.
8. Add in the broth.
9. Mix the ingredients carefully and cover the pan.
10. Add cilantro on top.
11. Your dish is ready to be served.

POLISH FRIED FISH

Preparation Time: 10 minutes
Cooking Time: 30 minutes
Serving: 2

Ingredients:

- Cod fillets, one pound
- Orange juice, one tablespoon
- Garlic powder, one teaspoon
- Lemon juice, half cup
- Bread crumbs, one cup
- Egg, one
- Chili powder, half tablespoon
- Olive oil, one cup
- Cilantro, one tablespoon
- Chopped parsley, as required
- Salt to taste
- Pepper to taste
- Cooking oil, as required

Directions:

1. Wash the cod filets and let them dry.
2. Take a small bowl.

3. Add orange juice, garlic powder, and lemon juice into the bowl.
4. Add chili powder and pepper.
5. Then add cilantro and mix them all well.
6. Add all the ingredients together to form a smooth paste.
7. Beat the eggs into a separate bowl.
8. Add the cod fillets into the mixture and coat well.
9. Dip the cod fillets into the egg mixture.
10. Coat the fillets in the bread crumbs.
11. Deep fry the cod filets.
12. Dish out your fish when it turns golden brown.
13. Add fresh chopped parsley on top.
14. Your dish is ready to be served.

POLISH BROCCOLI

Preparation Time: 10 minutes
Cooking Time: 20 minutes
Serving: 4

Ingredients:

- Garlic, one tablespoon
- Bay leaves, one
- Allspice powder, two teaspoons
- Black pepper, one tablespoon
- Smoked bacon, one cup
- Terderstem, one cup
- Dried marjoram, one tablespoon
- Dried chilies, eight
- Smoked sausage, half cup
- Chopped red onion, half cup
- Broccoli florets, one pound
- Passata paste, one cup
- Vegetable oil, two tablespoons
- Chopped cilantro leaves to garnish
- Salt, to taste
- Mashed potatoes, one cup (for serving)

Directions:

1. Take a large pan.
2. Add the oil and onions into the pan.
3. Cook the onions until they turn soft and translucent.
4. Add the garlic into the pan.
5. Cook the mixture well.
6. Add the passata paste and spices.
7. Cook the mixture for five minutes.
8. Add the smoked bacon and sausage to the pan.
9. Cook the ingredients well.

10. Add the rest of the ingredients.
11. Cover the pan and cook for ten minutes.
12. Garnish the dish with chopped cilantro leaves and serve it with mashed potatoes on the side.
13. Your dish is ready to be served.

POLISH SMOTHERED CHICKEN RECIPE

Preparation Time: 30 minutes
Cooking Time: 15 minutes
Serving: 4

Ingredients:

- Portobello mushrooms, one cup
- Sliced mozzarella cheese, one cup
- Cajun seasoning, half cup
- Vegetable cream cheese, half cup
- Lemon juice, two tablespoons
- Bacon strips, one cup
- Skinless chicken breast, one pound
- Salt, as required
- Butter, two tablespoons
- Crushed black pepper, as required
- Oregano, one teaspoon
- Garlic powder, one teaspoon

Directions:

1. Take a large pan.
2. Add the butter and bacon slices to it.
3. Fry the bacon slices and then dish it out.
4. Add the chicken and garlic powder to the pan.
5. Add the Cajun seasoning into the pan.
6. Add the rest of the ingredients into the pan.
7. Cook the ingredients for ten to fifteen minutes.
8. Crumble the cooked bacon slices on top before serving.
9. Your dish is ready to be served.

BEER SAUSAGE

Preparation and Cooking Time: 1 hour

Serving: 4

Ingredients:

- 1 (12 fluid oz.) can or bottle beer
- Four red potatoes, quartered
- 1 tsp. Italian seasoning
- salt and ground black pepper to taste
- 1 (8 oz.) package baby carrots
- 1/2 yellow onion, chopped
- One lb. smoked kielbasa sausage, cut into 1-inch slices
- One small head cabbage, quartered

Directions:

1. Boil the beef in a big pot on medium heat. On the bottom of the pot, layer the potatoes and sprinkle black pepper, salt, and a bit of Italian seasoning on top of it.
2. Layer the baby carrots, onion, smoked sausage, and cabbage. Sprinkle pepper, salt, and a little more Italian seasoning in each layer. Now turn down the heat to low and simmer for about 45 minutes, cover until the veggies become soft.

CHOCOLATE BABKA

Preparation & Cooking Time: 1 hour 30 minutes
Serving: 14

Ingredients:

- 2 cups all-purpose flour
- 1/3 cup unsweetened cocoa powder
- 1 1/2 tsp. baking powder
- 3/4 tsp. baking soda

- 1 tsp. ground cinnamon
- 1/2 tsp. salt
- 1 cup unsalted butter
- 1 1/4 cups white sugar
- 1 tsp. vanilla extract
- Three eggs
- 1 cup sour cream
- 1 cup semisweet chocolate chips
- 1 cup chopped pecans
- 1/4 cup white sugar
- 1 tsp. ground cinnamon

Directions:

1. Set an oven to preheat at 175°C (350°F). Grease a 10-inch tube pan with butter. Sift the salt, 1 tsp. Then put aside cinnamon, baking soda, baking powder, cocoa, and flour.
2. By using an electric mixer on high speed, beat the 1 1/4 cup of sugar and butter in a medium bowl until it turns fluffy and light. Adjust the speed to medium and beat in the vanilla—beat eggs one by one. Mash the flour mixture alternately with the sour cream into the creamed mixture at low speed, starting and ending with the flour mixture. Beat only just until blended.
3. To make the topping: Mix the 1teaspoon of cinnamon, 1/4 cup sugar, pecans, and chocolate in a small bowl to create a crumb mixture. Pour half of the butter in the bottom of the prepared pan, then spread. Sprinkle half of the crumb mixture on top. Pour the leftover batter and top with the leftover crumb mixture; lightly pressing the crumbs to stick into the batter. Using a knife, gently yet quickly cut through the crumbs and batter in an up and down motion. Tap the pan gently once on a hard surface to let the batter settle.
4. Bake in the oven for 40 minutes. Use aluminum foil to cover the top of the cake. Keep on baking for 20 minutes more until a skewer/toothpick is inserted among the side of the pan and the tube comes out clean. Let the cake cool for 30 minutes in the pan on a wire rack. Gently loosen the cake from the pan's sides and flip it onto the rack to fully cool.

GRANDMOTHER'S POLISH CABBAGE AND NOODLES

Preparation and Cooking Time: 45 minutes
Serving: 4

Ingredients:

- 1/4 cup butter
- One head cabbage, cored and chopped
- One large onion, diced
- 1 (12 oz.) package farfalle (bow-tie) pasta
- 2 tbsps. water
- 1 1/2 cups cooked ham, cut into bite-size pieces
- Two pinches white sugar, or to taste

Directions:

1. In a big skillet, liquefy butter over medium-low heat; cook and mix onion and cabbage until really soft for about half an hour.

2. With lightly salted water, fill a big pot and bring to a rolling boil. Mix in bow tie pasta and bring back to a boil. Cook pasta for about 12 minutes till tender but still slightly firm to the bite. Drain thoroughly and reserve.
3. Into cabbage mixture, mix cooked ham and water; heat through. Mix in sugar thoroughly.
4. Slowly mix bow tie pasta into the ham and cabbage, heat through.

KIELBASA AND VEGGIES

Preparation & Cooking Time: 1 hour 15 minutes
Serving: 4

Ingredients:

- 1 (10 oz.) package frozen mixed vegetables, thawed
- Four small potatoes, peeled and chopped
- 1 (16 oz.) package Polish beef sausage, cut into 1/4-inch slices
- 1/4 cup butter, cut into pieces
- 1 tbsp. lemon pepper
- 1/4 cup shredded Cheddar cheese

Directions:

1. Preheat the oven to 375 degrees F.
2. On the bottom of a 9x13-in. Lightly greased baking dish spread mixed frozen veggies. Mix in sausage and potatoes—evenly cut pats of butter on the mixture. Sprinkle lemon pepper. Use aluminum foil to cover.
3. Bake for 50 minutes at above temp. Carefully open foil. Put cheese on top; let it melt.

LAZY MAN'S PIEROGI

Preparation time: 10 minutes

Cooking time: 50 minutes

Servings: 6

Ingredients:

- 1 (16 oz.) package rotelle pasta
- 1/2 lb. bacon, chopped
- Two onions, chopped
- 1/2 lb. mushrooms, quartered
- 1 tbsp. butter
- 1 (16 oz.) can sauerkraut - rinsed and drained
- 2 (10.75 oz.) cans mushroom soup condensed cream
- salt and pepper to taste

Directions:

1. Boil a big pot of lightly salted water. Put in the pasta and cook until al dente or for 8-10 minutes. Set an oven to preheat at 175°C (350°F).
2. In a deep, big frying pan, put the bacon. Cook the bacon on medium-high heat until it browns evenly. Add onions and cook until it turns translucent. Sauté the mushrooms in butter in another pan.

3. Mix the condensed soup, sauerkraut, mushrooms, onion, bacon, and pasta in a big bowl. Sprinkle pepper and salt to season. Pour the mixture into a 9x13-inch baking dish.
4. Bake in the oven for 45 minutes.

POLISH PIEROGIES WITH POTATOES AND CHEESE

Preparation time: 10 minutes

Cooking time: 50 minutes

Servings: 6

Ingredients for the filling:

- Five potatoes
- 8 ounces of farmer's cheese
- 1 Tbsp. of blue cheese, optional
- 2 Tbsp. of cheddar cheese, shredded
- One onion, whole and chopped
- ½ tsp. of powdered garlic
- ½ tsp. of powdered onion
- 1 Tbsp. of oil
- Dash of salt and black pepper

Ingredients for the dough:

- 3 cups of all-purpose flour
- ½ cup of warm whole milk ½ to ¾ cup of warm water
- 1 Tbsp. of melted butter
- Dash of salt
- Ingredients for toppings:
- One onion, chopped
- Three slices of bacon, cooked and chopped
- ½ cup of sour cream
- 2 Tbsp. of vegetable oil, for frying

Directions:

1. Place a large pot over medium to high heat. Fill with water and boil. Add in the potatoes and boil for 15 to 20 minutes or soft.
2. Place a large skillet over medium heat. Add the oil, and once hot, add in the onions. Cook for 5 minutes or until golden brown.
3. Add the farmer's cheese, cheddar cheese, powdered garlic, and powdered onion—season with a dash of salt and black pepper. Stir well until evenly incorporated.
4. Add the flour into the center of a flat surface. Add the dash of salt, warm milk, melted butter. Add in a touch of water and stir well to mix until a dough begins to form. Now spread the dough into a ball and cover. Set aside to rest for 10 to 15 minutes.
5. Roll out the dough until ¼ inch in thickness. Use a wine glass and cut out circles from the dough.
6. Place a tsp of the filling into the center of each circle of dough.

7. Wet half of the dough circle with water and fold over the filling. To seal the edges, crimp them with a fork. Repeat with the remaining dough circles and filling.
8. Place a large pot over medium heat. Fill with water and boil. Add in the pierogies.
9. Pull from the oven and place on a platter lined with paper towels to drain.
10. Serve with a topping of chopped onion, bacon, and sour cream.

POLISH GROUND MEAT ROAST

Preparation Time: 20 minutes
Cooking Time: 10 minutes
Serving: 4

Ingredients:

- Fresh chopped cilantro, three tablespoons
- Salt, to taste
- Black pepper, to taste
- Lemon spice mix, two tablespoons
- Red wine, half cup
- Ground pork meat, one and a half pound
- Horseradish, one teaspoon
- Dried marjoram, one cup
- Caraway seeds, two tablespoons
- Ground beef meat, one and a half pound
- Ground veal meat, one pound
- Olive oil, one tablespoon
- Mixed cheese, two cups

Directions:

1. In a large mixing basin, combine all of the ingredients.
2. Mix everything thoroughly, making sure the meat is well-coated with the marinade.
3. Preheat an oven.
4. Lay the meat on a baking tray.
5. Also enure the baking tray is greased properly.
6. Add the cheese on top.
7. Roast the meat for 10 to 15 minutes.
8. Garnish the dish with fresh chopped cilantro.
9. The dish is ready to be served.

POLISH PORK ROAST WITH WINE RECIPE

Cooking Time: 10 minutes

Preparation Time: 20 minutes
Serving: 4

Ingredients:

- Fresh chopped cilantro, three tablespoons

- Salt, to taste
- Black pepper, to taste
- Lemon spice mix, two tablespoons
- Red wine, half cup
- Pork meat, one and a half pound
- Horseradish, one teaspoon
- Dried marjoram, one cup
- Caraway seeds, two tablespoons
- Olive oil, one tablespoon

Directions:

1. Add the listed ingredients to a large bowl.
2. Mix everything properly and make sure the pork meat is coated with the marinade.
3. Preheat an oven.
4. Lay the pork meat on a baking tray.
5. Enure the baking tray is greased properly.
6. Roast the pork meat for ten to fifteen minutes.
7. Garnish the dish with fresh chopped cilantro.
8. The dish is ready to be served.

POLISH BAKED SALMON

Serving: 2

Preparation Time: 10 minutes
Cooking Time: 25 minutes

Ingredients:

- Smoked paprika, half teaspoon
- Powdered cumin, one tablespoon
- Black pepper, to taste
- Salt, to taste
- Turmeric powder, one teaspoon
- Onion, one cup

- Dijon mustard, half cup
- Salmon pieces, one pound
- Minced garlic, two tablespoons
- Minced ginger, two tablespoons
- Cilantro, half cup
- Olive oil, two tablespoons
- All-purpose flour, three tablespoons

Directions:

1. Take a large bowl.
2. Add the oil and onions into the bowl.
3. Add the chopped garlic and ginger to the bowl.
4. Add the tomatoes to the bowl.
5. Add the spices.
6. Add the cilantro to it.
7. Mix all the ingredients.
8. Add the all-purpose flour and mix the ingredients.
9. Cover the salmon pieces with the mixture above.
10. Bake the salmon pieces.
11. Dish them out when cooked properly.
12. Sprinkle some cilantro and sliced almond on top.
13. You can serve it with any of your preferred sauces.
14. Your dish is ready to be served.

POLISH MEAT CUTLETS RECIPE

Cooking Time: 15 minutes

Preparation Time: 25 minutes
Serving: 4

Ingredients:

- Chopped garlic, two teaspoons
- Chopped red onions, three tablespoons
- Chopped cilantro, half cup
- Minced veal meat, two cups
- Chopped fresh dill, two tablespoons
- Vegetable oil, two tablespoons
- Salt to taste
- Minced turkey meat, two cups
- Black pepper to taste
- Eggs, two
- Butter, two teaspoons

Directions:

1. Add the onions and the garlic to a large bowl.

2. Add in the rest of the ingredients except the eggs.
3. Make round cutlets from the mixture.
4. Heat the oil and butter in a pan.
5. Beat the eggs in a bowl.
6. Dip the cutlets in the egg mixture.
7. Fry the meat cutlets.
8. Dish the cutlets out when the patties turn golden brown on both sides.
9. Add cilantro on top.
10. The dish is ready to be served.

POLISH ROASTED GRILLED RIBS RECIPE

Cooking Time: 10 minutes

Preparation Time: 20 minutes
Serving: 4

Ingredients:

- Fresh chopped cilantro, three tablespoons
- Salt, to taste
- Black pepper, to taste
- Lemon spice mix, two tablespoons
- Red wine, half cup
- Beef meat, one and a half pound
- Horseradish, one teaspoon
- Dried marjoram, one cup
- Caraway seeds, two tablespoons
- Small potatoes, half-pound
- Olive oil, one tablespoon

Directions:

1. Add the ingredients to a large bowl.
2. Mix everything properly and make sure the ribs are coated with the marinade.
3. Preheat a grilling pan.
4. Place the ribs on a grilling pan.
5. Make sure you grease the pan with butter properly.
6. Grill the ribs for ten to fifteen minutes on both sides.
7. Garnish the dish with fresh chopped cilantro.
8. The dish is ready to be served.

POLISH FISH WITH ROOT VEGETABLES RECIPE

Cooking Time: 25 minutes

Preparation Time: 10 minutes

Serving: 2

Ingredients:

- Onion, one cup
- Powdered cumin, one tablespoon
- Black pepper, to taste
- Salt, to taste
- Turmeric powder, one teaspoon
- Smoked paprika, half teaspoon
- Fish filet pieces, one pound
- Minced garlic, two tablespoons
- Root vegetables, two cups
- Minced ginger, two tablespoons
- Cilantro, half cup
- Olive oil, two tablespoons

Directions:

1. Take a large bowl.
2. Add the oil and onions into the bowl.
3. Add the chopped garlic and ginger to the bowl.
4. Add the spices.
5. Add the cilantro to it.
6. Mix all the ingredients.
7. Add the fish pieces with the mixture into a pan.
8. Cook the fish pieces.
9. Add the root vegetables into the pan.
10. Dish them out when cooked properly.
11. Sprinkle some cilantro on top.
12. Your dish is ready to be served.

KIELBASA AND CABBAGE PIEROGIES

Preparation time: 10 minutes

Cooking time: 50 minutes

Servings: 6

Ingredients:

- One pack of pierogies, frozen
- One pack of kielbasa
- One head of cabbage, fresh
- One onion, thinly sliced
- Dash of salt and black pepper
- ¼ cup of water
- 1 Tbsp. of vegetable oil
- 1 Tbsp. of butter

Directions:

1. Place a large skillet over medium heat. Fill with water and boil.
2. Add in the pack of pierogies. Once they begin to float to the surface, drain and set aside on a plate lined with paper towels to drain.
3. In the same skillet, add in the oil. Once it is hot enough, add in the kielbasa—Cook for 8 to 10 minutes or brown.
4. Add in the shredded cabbage and add in the water.
5. Cover and steam for 12 to 15 minutes. Remove and transfer to a plate.
6. In that skillet, add in the butter. Once melted, add in the pierogies—Cook for 2 to 3 minutes on each side or until browned.
7. Add to the plate the cabbage and kielbasa. Serve.

BACON AND PIEROGI BAKE

Preparation time: 10 minutes

Cooking time: 30 minutes

Servings: 6

Ingredients:

- 1, 16-ounce pack of potato and cheddar pierogies, frozen
- Four slices of bacon, chopped
- Two cloves of garlic, minced
- 1, 8-ounce pack of cream cheese, soft
- ½ cup of chicken broth
- Dash of salt and black pepper
- 1 cup of cheddar cheese, shredded
- 2 to 3 green onions, chopped
- ¼ cup of plum tomato, seeds removed and chopped

Directions:

1. Preheat the oven to 400 degrees. Place the pierogies into a large baking dish.
2. Place a medium skillet over medium heat. Add in the bacon slices and cook for 8 to 10 minutes or crispy. Remove and transfer to a large plate lined with a sheet of paper towels.
3. In the same skillet with the bacon drippings, add the garlic—Cook for 30 seconds before adding in the cream cheese. Stir well until it starts to melt.
4. Gently pour in the chicken broth and stir well until smooth inconsistency. Season with a dash of salt and black pepper.
5. Pour the sauce over the pierogies in the baking dish. And
6. place into the oven to bake for 15 minutes or until bubbly.
7. Take out of the oven and top off with the shredded cheddar cheese. Put back into the oven to bake for 5 minutes or until the cheese is melted.
8. Remove and serve with the cooked bacon, chopped green onions, and tomatoes.

Preparation time: 10 minutes

Cooking time: 60 minutes

Servings: 3

Ingredients:

- 1, 16-ounce pack of potato and onion pierogies
- 1 Tbsp. of water
- 1, 7-ounce pack of kielbasa sausage, thinly sliced
- 1, a 4-ounce container of cream cheese, soft
- ½ cup of sour cream
- ½ cup of chicken broth
- 1/8 tsp. of black pepper
- 1 cup of cheddar cheese, shredded
- ½ cup of green onions, thinly sliced

Directions:

1. Preheat the oven to 375 degrees. Coat a large baking dish with cooking spray.
2. Place the pierogies and water into a medium bowl—cover and microwave for 2 minutes. Stir and continue to microwave for 1 ½ to 2 minutes.
3. Next, put the pierogies into the baking dish. Top them off with the kielbasa sausage slices.
4. Add in the soft cream cheese, sour cream, chicken broth, and black pepper in a medium bowl. Whisk until smooth inconsistency. Add half a cup of the cheddar cheese and 1/3of the sliced green onions. Stir well to incorporate.
5. Pour the cream cheese mixture over the top. Cover the baking dish with a sheet of aluminum foil.
6. Place into the oven to bake for 23 to 28 minutes or until cooked through.
7. Remove the aluminum foil. Top off with the remaining cheddar cheese. Place back into the oven to bake for 5 minutes or until the cheese is melted.
8. Remove and serve immediately with the green onions.

SAUSAGE PIEROGI SKILLET

Preparation time: 10 minutes

Cooking time: 40 minutes

Servings: 2

Ingredients:

- Five chicken and apple sausage links, sliced thinly
- 32 ounces of pierogies, frozen and thawed
- Two green bell peppers, sliced into strips
- 6 to 8 Tbsp. of butter, evenly divided
- 3 to 6 Tbsp. of extra virgin olive oil
- 2 cups of chicken stock
- 3 Tbsp. of all-purpose flour
- 2 Tbsp. of whole grain mustard
- ¼ to ½ cup of heavy cream
- 1 cup of mozzarella cheese, grated

Directions:

1. Preheat the oven to 425 degrees.
2. Place a large skillet over medium heat. Add in three tablespoons of the butter, and once melted, add in the olive oil. Once hot, add in the pierogies—Cook for 2 to 3 minutes or until browned. Turn and continue to cook for another 2 to 3 minutes or until browned on the other side. Remove from the skillet and set aside.
3. In the same skillet, add another tbsp of butter and olive oil. Once hot, add in the sausage links—Cook for 8 to 10 minutes or until cooked through.
4. Add in the red bell peppers and continue to cook for 5 minutes or until soft. Remove and transfer to a plate. Set aside.
5. Add three tablespoons of butter into the skillet. Once melted, add in the all-purpose flour and continue to cook for 2 minutes or until golden brown. Pour in the chicken stock and mustard. Whisk until smooth inconsistency.
6. Add in the heavy cream and simmer for 2 to 3 minutes or until thick inconsistency.
7. Add the pierogies into the skillet and stir well to coat.
8. Sprinkle the grated mozzarella cheese over the top.
9. Place into the oven to bake for 10 to 15 minutes or until the cheese is melted.
10. Remove and serve immediately.

PIEROGI WITH SAUERKRAUT AND DRIED MUSHROOMS

Preparation and Cooking Time: 1 hour 32 minutes

Serving: 5
Ingredients:

- 1 cup water to cover
- 1/4 cup dried mushrooms

- 1 tbsp. olive oil
- One onion, chopped
- 2 cups sauerkraut - drained, rinsed, and finely chopped
- salt and ground black pepper to taste

Dough:

- 4 cups all-purpose flour
- One egg
- 1 cup lukewarm water
- 3 tbsps. melted butter

Directions:

1. Mix the dried mushrooms and 1 cup water on low heat in a saucepan and let it simmer. Cook for approx. 10 minutes, or until soft. Drain the mushrooms and set aside the cooking water. Chop the mushrooms.
2. In a separate pan, heat the olive oil over medium heat. and cook the onion for about 5 minutes until it turns translucent and tender. Put in sauerkraut and mushrooms and stir well. Sprinkle pepper and salt to season. Pour the reserved cooking water, cover, then simmer for 15-20 minutes until the sauerkraut turns soft and the water evaporates.
3. In a big bowl, put the flour and make a well in the middle. Into the well, crack the egg, and pour enough warm water, 1 tbsp at a time, until it forms a dough, while continuously stirring with your hands. Knead the dough well and keep on adding more water as necessary. Knead the dough until it is smooth and soft.
4. Use flour to dust a work surface. Slice off 1/4 of the dough and roll it out to 1/8-inch thick. Using a round pastry cutter or a glass to cut out circles.
5. Put in 1 tsp. Of sauerkraut filling to fill each circle of dough. Fold the dough over into a half-moon shape and secure the edges. Use a clean dish towel to cover so the pierogi will not dry out. Redo the process with the rest of the filling and dough.
6. Boil a big pan of salted water gently. Put the pierogi in batches and cook for 5-7 minutes until they float into the surface. Once they float into the surface, cook for 2-3 minutes more. Take it out using a slotted spoon, then drizzle in melted butter.

POLISH BEEF SOUP WITH LIVER BALLS

Preparation and Cooking Time: 45 minutes

Serving: 4
Ingredients:

- 1 cup ground chicken liver
- 1 cup dried bread crumbs
- 3 tbsps. all-purpose flour
- Two eggs
- 1/4 tbsp. chopped fresh parsley
- 1 tsp. salt
- 1/8 tsp. dried marjoram
- 1/8 tsp. ground mace

- One clove garlic, minced
- 2 lbs. short rib steaks
- Two onions, thinly sliced
- Three stalks chopped celery, with leaves
- 4 tsp. salt
- 3/4 tsp. ground black pepper
- 8 cups water
- Two carrots halved
- Three tomatoes, chopped
- Four sprigs of fresh parsley

Directions:

1. Mix the garlic, mace, marjoram, 1 tsp thoroughly—salt, parsley, eggs, flour, bread crumbs, and liver. Allow the meatball mixture to stand.
2. Wash the ribs and put them in a big stockpot. Put the parsley, tomatoes, carrots, water, pepper, 4 tsp: salt, celery, and onions. Put cover, then let it boil. Remove the foam from the surface of the soup, then simmer for 1 1/2 hours until the meat is tender.
3. Take out the carrots, bones, and meat from the soup. Slice the carrots and meat into bite-sized pieces, then put them back into the soup. Let it boil.
4. Form the meatball mixture into balls similar to the size of golf balls, then put it in the soup. Put the cover and cook for 10 minutes.

POLISH CHICKEN AND DUMPLINGS

Preparation and Cooking Time: 3 hours 30 minutes

Serving: 8
Ingredients:

- 1 (3 lb.) whole chicken
- One onion, chopped
- One stalk celery, with leaves
- 1 tbsp. poultry seasoning
- 1 tsp. whole allspice
- 1 tsp. dried basil
- 1/2 tsp. salt
- 1 tsp. black pepper
- 1 tsp. seasoning salt
- 1 (10.75 oz.) can chicken soup condensed cream o(optional)

DUMPLINGS:

- Four eggs
- 2 tbsps. olive oil
- 1 tbsp. salt
- 1 tsp. black pepper
- 2 cups water
- 4 cups all-purpose flour

Directions:

1. Put the celery, onion, and chicken in a big pot, then pour water to fill the pot. Sprinkle with seasoning salt, 1 tsp. Pepper, 1/2 tsp. Salt, basil, whole allspice, and poultry season, then boil. Turn down the heat to low and continue to cook until the chicken is cooked through, about 2 hours.
2. Take out the chicken from the broth and strain the broth to remove any bone or seasonings. Put back the broth into the pan, mix in cream of chicken soup and keep on simmering. Put chicken aside to cool.
3. Mix the 2 cups of water with 1 tsp. Pepper, 1 tbsp. Salt, olive oil, and eggs together in a medium bowl. Gently add in the flour mixture until it becomes thick.
4. Scoop a spoonful of the dough using a knife and a big spoon, then cut little pieces into the broth. Stir and simmer for about 15 minutes with cover. Redo the steps until the rest of the dough has been used.
5. In the meantime, take out the bone and skin of the chicken. Slice the meat into little pieces, stir into the broth, heat it through; serve.

POLISH MEAT AND POTATOES

Preparation and Cooking Time: 50 minutes

Serving: 4
Ingredients:

- Four potatoes, peeled and cut into 1-inch cubes
- One onion, chopped
- Two green bell peppers, cut into 1-inch pieces
- 1/2 tsp. onion powder
- 1/2 tsp. garlic powder
- 1/2 tsp. salt
- 1/4 tsp. black pepper
- 1/4 cup vegetable oil
- 1 (16 oz.) package kielbasa sausage, cut into 1-inch pieces

Directions:

1. In a big pan, heat the oil on medium-high heat. Cook the potatoes and onions for 15 minutes while stirring once in a while. Minimize the heat to medium and stir in the pepper, salt, garlic powder, onion powder, and bell pepper.
2. Cook for 5 minutes with cover. Mix in kielbasa and cook with cover until onions are caramelized or for 15 minutes.

POLISH NOODLES

Preparation and Cooking Time: 55 minutes

Serving: 8
Ingredients:

- 1 (8 oz.) package kluski noodles
- 2 (12 oz.) packages sage pork sausage
- One green pepper, diced
- One onion, diced
- 4 cups water, or as needed

- One large head cabbage, chopped
- salt and pepper to taste
- 1/2 cup sour cream (optional)

Directions:

1. Bring the pot of slightly salted water to a rolling boil on high heat. Stir in the egg noodles, then boil again. Cook for about 5 minutes without cover, stirring from time to time until the pasta is firm to the bite yet cooked through. Drain it.
2. In the meantime, on medium-high heat, heat a big pan and stir in the onion, green pepper, and sausage. Cook and stir for about 10 minutes until the sausage is not pink, browned evenly, and crumbly. Let it drain and get rid of the excess grease.
3. In a big pot, boil 4 cups of water—mix in the noodles, sausage mixture, and cabbage. Simmer for about 30 minutes on medium-low heat, stirring once in a while, until the cabbage becomes soft. If needed, pour in water while cooking; the mixture must not be dry. Put pepper and salt to season. If preferred, put sour cream on top as garnish.

POLISH PIEROGIES WITH CABBAGE AND MUSHROOM SAUCE

Preparation time: 10 minutes

Cooking time: 60 minutes

Servings: 7

Ingredients: Dough:

- 1 tbsp. butter
- 1 cup water
- 3 cups of all-purpose flour, plus more for surface

Filling:

- One medium head cabbage, quartered
- One onion, finely chopped
- 3 tbsps. olive oil
- 1 tsp. caraway seeds
- 1 tsp. salt
- 1 tsp. ground black pepper
- Mushroom Sauce:
- 3/4 cup dried mushrooms
- 2 cups sliced fresh mushrooms
- One onion
- 3 tbsps. heavy cream
- 1 tbsp. potato starch
- salt and pepper to taste

Directions:

1. Mix 1/3 of the water and butter in a pan, then boil; stir in leftover water.

2. In a bowl, sift in the flour, then add the water-butter mixture and stir. To form a smooth dough, knead the mixture for 5 minutes, place it on a plate and cover with an inverted bowl. Let it rest for 30 minutes.
3. In a pot, lay the quartered cabbage, pour water to cover, and boil it for about 15 minutes until it becomes soft. Gently press to remove as much liquid as possible. Drain it, and using a clean kitchen towel, wrap the cabbage.
4. Slice into thin slices the dry cabbage and place it in a bowl. Stir onion and sprinkle with pepper, salt, and caraway to season. Cook for about 10 minutes in a non-stick skillet until it becomes soft. Stir in onions and fresh mushrooms, then cook for 10 minutes more. Mix the potato starch and cream in a cup, then add it to the mushrooms. Let it boil and put pepper and salt to season. On a floured surface, spread about 1/4 of the dough, about 1/16-inch thick, and by using a glass or a cookie cutter, cut rounds of about 3 1/2 inches across. Add the remaining dough into the other 1/4 of the dough and repeat the steps.
5. In the middle of each dough round, put about 1 tsp. Of the cabbage filling, then fold it into a half-moon shape, pressing and securing the edges using a fork. Put the filled pierogies aside beneath a towel to avoid drying.
6. Boil a big pan of water and drop about 15 pieces of pierogies at a time into the boiling water. Cook in simmering water for about 5-10 minutes until it floats into the top. Cook the leftover pierogies in batches with the same process.

GREEK STYLE POLISH FISH

Preparation time: 15min
Cooking time: 30min

Servings: 4

Ingredients:

- 1 lb. Fish fillets (walleye, pike, perch, tilapia, etc., any white fish)
- Black pepper and salt to taste
- ½ cup Flour
- 2 tbsp. oil
- For the Veggies:
- 4 tbsp. Tomato paste
- 1 Bay leaf
- 5-6 whole allspice
- One leek, sliced
- 1 Parsnip, grated (peeled)
- 1 Celery rib, grated
- Two carrots, grated (peeled)
- 2 tbsp. Oil
- Black pepper and salt to taste

Directions:

1. Rinse the fish and pat dry. Now season with black pepper and salt to taste. Coat with flour.
2. Place a skillet over medium and add oil. Cook the fish until it becomes golden brown. Set aside.
3. In the meantime, in another skillet, add 2 tbsp—oil over medium. Once heated, add the leek, parsnip, celery, and carrots. Sauté for 10 minutes. Add tomato paste, bay leaf, and allspice. Simmer until tender and until the liquid evaporates. Discard allspice and bay leaf—season with black pepper and salt to taste.
4. Serve the fish on top of the veggie mixture. Top with more veggie mixture.
5. Serve cold or hot and enjoy!

GRILLED KIELBASA AND SAUERKRAUT

Preparation time: 10min
Cooking time: 25min

Servings: 4

Ingredients:

- 1 ½ lb. Polska kielbasa, smoked
- 2 tbsp. Butter
- 3 tbsp. Sugar
- 3 cups drained Sauerkraut
- One sliced Onion
- 3 tbsp. Parsley, chopped
- Honey Mustard Sauce
- Honey Mustard Sauce:
- ½ tsp. Cayenne
- ¼ cup of Dijon mustard
- ¼ cup of Honey
- ¼ cup of Yellow Mustard
- 1 tbsp. prepared Horseradish
- 1/8 tsp. Salt
- 1/8 tsp. Black pepper

Directions:

1. Preheating the grill and the oven, 400F.
2. Cut Polska kielbasa into lengths (3-inch) and cut lengthwise. Now cook on the grill for 5 minutes per side. Transfer in a baking sheet—Cook in the oven for five more minutes.
3. Turn on medium-high heat and place a skillet on the stove. Add the sugar and butter. Let it cook until golden brown. Then add the onion. Cook to caramelize. Add the sauerkraut—cook5 minutes.
4. Remove the kielbasa from the oven. Cut into pieces (1-inch). Add it to the skillet with the sauerkraut. Toss to combine and cook for 1 minute.
5. Make the sauce. In a bowl, combine all ingredients. Mix well.
6. Serve on a plate and garnish with chopped parsley. Serve with the sauce. Enjoy!

STUFFED CABBAGE

Preparation time: 10 minutes

Cooking time: 40 minutes

Servings: 6

Ingredients:

- 1/2 medium cabbage
- 4 cups of sauerkraut
- One can of tomato paste

- 500g sliced bacon
- 500g diced pork meat
- 500g sliced sausage
- One large onion, diced
- Two garlic cloves
- One bay leaf
- Salt
- Pepper

Directions:

1. Cut your washed cabbage into thin slices and boil until tender in a pot.
2. Boil the sauerkraut in another pot in about 2 cups of water.
3. Strain and keep the sour water aside.
4. Fry your diced pork in a pan, then set aside.
5. Cook the bacon and sausage with the onion and garlic in a skillet.
6. In a large saucepan, combine the cooked cabbage, sauerkraut, sour water, tomato paste, spices, and cooked meats, onion, and garlic.
7. Boil for about 1 hour.
8. Serve.

CABBAGE ROLLS

Preparation time: 10 minutes

Cooking time: 30 minutes

Servings: 8

Ingredients:

- One head of cabbage
- 1kg beef mincemeat
- 1kg pork mincemeat
- 2 cups of cooked rice
- Two eggs
- Four garlic cloves
- One large onion
- Two tablespoons of butter
- Two tablespoons of marjoram
- One teaspoon of marjoram
- One tablespoon of thyme
- One teaspoon of salt
- One teaspoon of pepper
- Two cans of crushed tomatoes
- One can of tomato sauce

Directions:

1. Fry minced garlic and chopped onion in butter until golden.
2. Beat two eggs with marjoram, thyme, salt, and pepper in a bowl mix mincemeat, rice, onion, garlic, and eggs. Mix it well. Cover it and let it sit in the fridge.
3. Core cabbage.
4. Blanche cabbage leaves in boiling water, peeling them off as they become limp. Once leaves are separated, cut off stems (centers).
5. Put about 2 tbsp of filling in the center of each leaf.
6. Fold the sides of the leaf in and roll it up into a little package. Put rolls in casserole. Pour rolls with all cans of tomatoes.
7. Sprinkle with marjoram.
8. Bake at 180°C for 2 hours.
9. Serve.

DUCK WITH APPLES

Preparation time: 10 minutes

Cooking time: 40 minutes

Servings: 7

Ingredients:

- Duck
- 1 1/2 teaspoon salt
- One teaspoon pepper
- 1/2 teaspoon garlic powder
- 1/2 teaspoon paprika
- Five small apples
- 1/4 cup honey
- 1/4 cup fresh orange juice, strained
- Two tablespoons lemon juice, strained

Directions:

1. In a small bowl, combine the garlic powder, salt, pepper, and paprika.
2. Remove the duck's insides, then wash and pat it dry. Rub the spice and salt mixture all over the duck, inside and out.
3. Cut the apples in half and core them.
4. Stuff the duck with as many apples as you can. Then, using kitchen thread, knot the drumsticks together.
5. Place the duck on a roasting pan, upside down.
6. Combine the honey, orange juice, and lemon juice in a mixing bowl. And glaze the duck.
7. Roast at 180°C for 1 hour.

POLISH MEATBALLS

Preparation time: 10 minutes

Cooking time: 30 minutes

Servings: 3

Ingredients:

- 300g ground beef chuck
- 200g lean ground pork
- One slice of stale white bread
- 1/4 cup milk
- One small finely chopped onion
- One large, slightly beaten egg
- Two tablespoons breadcrumbs
- Two tablespoons beef stock or water
- Salt and pepper to taste
- Mushroom Sauce:
- 40g porcini mushrooms
- 200g fresh sliced mushrooms
- Two tablespoons all-purpose flour
- 2 cups boiling water
- Two tablespoons butter
- One chopped onion
- One teaspoon chicken base
- 1 cup sour cream
- Salt and pepper to taste

Directions:

1. Soak bread in a large bowl in the milk until it is soft. Add beef, pork, onion, egg, salt, pepper, and mix it all together thoroughly. If the mixture is too mushy, add 1 to 2 tablespoons of breadcrumbs. Also, in order make sure your seasonings are correct, fry a tiny patty and taste and adjust as necessary.
2. Heat the oven to 150°C. Use a medium scoop and portion out meatballs, giving them one final roll with dampened hands.
3. Coat a skillet with cooking spray and use it to brown the meatballs on all sides. Transfer it to a baking pan with a lip, add two tablespoons of water or stock, and bake, uncovered, for 30 minutes.
4. Sauce: Place dried mushrooms in a heat-resistant bowl and pour 2 cups of boiling water in and then let it steep 30 minutes.
5. Sauté one large chopped onion in butter in a medium saucepan until caramelized. Add mushrooms to the saucepan once the onions are translucent.
6. Add chicken base and then bring it to a boil, reduce the heat, and simmer while the pot is covered for 30 minutes.
7. A fork blends two tablespoons of flour into sour cream in a medium bowl. Temper the sour cream by adding three ladles of hot mushroom liquid, while whisking until smooth.
8. Next, slowly pour the tempered sour cream into the mushroom sauce while constantly whisking.
9. Simmer for 5-10 minutes until thickened and the taste of the raw flour is cooked out.

10. The cooked meatballs can then be put in this sauce, reheated, and then served over noodles, mashed potatoes, or rice.

KOTLER MELONY

Preparation time: 10 minutes

Cooking time: 30 minutes

Servings: 4

Ingredients:

- 500g minced meat
- Five garlic cloves
- 100ml water
- One onion
- Flour
- Breadcrumbs
- Marjoram
- Cumin
- Parsley
- Black pepper
- Oil
- Salt

Directions:

1. Mix meat with water and leave it for 30 minutes.
2. Dice onion.
3. Add onion, egg, pepper, cumin, marjoram, garlic, parsley, salt, flour, and breadcrumbs. Mix it well and shape small flattened balls.
4. Fry in oil on both sides.
5. Serve with potatoes.

KOTLER SCHABOWY

Preparation time: 10 minutes

Cooking time: 30 minutes

Servings: 4

Ingredients:

- Four medium pork chops
- 60g flour
- 1/4 teaspoon garlic powder
- 1/4 teaspoon dried marjoram

- One egg, beaten
- One tablespoon oil
- One tablespoon butter
- Salt and pepper

Directions:

1. Pound the pork chops until they are fairly thin. Then season with salt, pepper, garlic powder, and marjoram. Next, set it aside.
2. On separate plates pour the flour and egg.
3. Dip each chop into the flour so that you coat both sides. Then dip into the beaten egg and then back into the flour so that it has an even coating.
4. Heat both the oil and butter in a large frying pan. Add the pork and cook it on high heat for about 3-5 minutes on each side.
5. Finally, lower your heat and cook for another few minutes until it is golden.
6. Serve with cooked potatoes.

BAKED SALMON

Preparation time: 10 minutes

Cooking time: 30 minutes

Servings: 3

Ingredients:

- Two salmon fillets, boneless, without skin
- Two garlic cloves
- 30g butter
- One tablespoon chopped fresh dill
- 1/2 teaspoon crushed black peppercorns
- One tablespoon lemon juice
- One tablespoon water/stock/dry white wine
- One bay leaf, deveined and snipped in slices
- Salt

Directions:

1. Preheat oven to 200°C.
2. Wash and pat the salmon dry and place skin side down, in the middle of an aluminum foil large enough to fold over in a slight tent shape.
3. Place all the other ingredients in a bowl and mix thoroughly.
4. Spread the paste on one fillet and place the other fillet over it.
5. Pull both sides of the foil up and seal the top and sides, leaving a little space at the top for the salmon to steam.
6. Bake in the oven for 20-25 minutes.
7. Serve with potatoes and cucumber salad.

Preparation time: 10 minutes

Cooking time: 40 minutes

Servings: 6

Ingredients:

- 100g salami
- 250g sausage
- Two onions
- Two tablespoons of sweet paprika
- 1kg potatoes
- One tablespoon of crushed cumin
- 50ml oil
- 125ml cooking cream
- Salt

Directions:

1. Cook boil potatoes.
2. Meanwhile, fry onion in oil.
3. Add diced potatoes, spice, salt, sliced sausage, salami, and fry it for a while.
4. Pour some water, add salt and boil for 30 minutes.
5. Serve with fresh bread, dumplings, or potato pancakes

MEAT STUFFED POTATO DUMPLINGS

Preparation time: 10 minutes

Cooking time: 40 minutes

Servings: 4

Ingredients:

- 250g smoked meat
- 100g cottage cheese
- 700g potatoes
- 150g flour
- 80g breadcrumbs
- 100g semolina
- One onion
- Two eggs
- Oil
- Salt
- Sauerkraut

Directions:

1. Boil meat for 1 hour and potatoes for 30 minutes.
2. Dice meat and fry with onion in oil.
3. Peel and grate potatoes. Mix them with breadcrumbs, flour, semolina, salt, and whipped eggs. Make a dough and roll it 1cm thick. Cut squares.
4. Mix meat, onion, and cheese. Spoon the mixture in the middle of each one and make dumplings.
5. Boil them in saltwater for 20 minutes.
6. Serve with sauerkraut and fried onion.

POLISH BARANINA RECIPE

Cooking Time: 10 minutes

Preparation Time: 20 minutes
Serving: 4

Ingredients:

- Fresh chopped cilantro, three tablespoons
- Salt, to taste
- Black pepper, to taste
- Lemon spice mix, two tablespoons
- Capers, one tablespoon
- Mutton chops, one and a half pound
- Horseradish, one teaspoon
- Heavy cream, one cup
- Mayonnaise, two tablespoons

- Dry white wine, half cup
- Olive oil, one tablespoon

Directions:

1. At first add all the ingredients to a large bowl.
2. Mix everything correctly and make sure the mutton chops are coated with the marinade.
3. Preheat an oven.
4. Lay the mutton chops on a baking tray.
5. Ensure the baking tray is greased properly.
6. Roast the mutton chops for ten to fifteen minutes.
7. Garnish the chops with fresh chopped cilantro.
8. The dish is ready to be served.

POLISH HALUSKI RECIPE

Cooking Time: 15 minutes

Preparation Time: 30 minutes
Serving: 4

Ingredients:

- Egg noodles, one packet
- Sliced green cabbage, two cups
- Chopped parsley, half cup
- Chopped yellow onions, half cup
- Lemon juice, two tablespoons
- Grated cottage cheese, two tablespoons
- Bacon slices, one cup
- Salt, as required
- Butter, two tablespoons
- Crushed black pepper, as required

Directions:

1. Take a large pan.
2. Add the butter and bacon slices to it.
3. Fry the bacon slices and then dish it out.
4. Add the onions and cabbage into the pan.
5. Boil the noodles according to the package instructions in another saucepan.
6. Drain the noodles.
7. Add the noodles into the pan.
8. Add the left over ingredients into the pan.
9. Cook the ingredients for ten to fifteen minutes.
10. Crumble the cooked bacon slices on top before serving.
11. Your dish is ready to be served.

POLISH SAUERKRAUT AND MUSHROOM PIES

Cooking Time: 30 minutes

Preparation Time: 10 minutes
Serving: 4

Ingredients:

- Butter, half cup
- Chopped sauerkraut, two tablespoons
- Pie dough, as required
- Sliced mushrooms, half cup
- Salt, as required
- Black pepper, as required
- Mix spice, two teaspoons
- Parsley, half cup
- Butter, for greasing
- Minced garlic, one teaspoon

Directions:

1. Add the butter to a large pan.
2. Add the spices and garlic to the pan.
3. Add the sauerkraut and sliced mushrooms when the garlic changes color.
4. Cook the ingredients well.
5. Lay the pie dough into a greased pie dish.
6. Add the sauerkraut and mushroom mixture on top.
7. Bake the dish properly for 10-15 minutes.
8. Garnish the dish with chopped parsley.
9. The dish is ready to be served.

MUSHROOM APPLE PIEROGIES

Cooking Time: 40 minutes

Preparation Time: 20 minutes
Serving: 4

Ingredients:

- ¼ cup smooth or chunky applesauce
- 1 tbsp. vegetable oil
- Two eggs
- 1 tsp. kosher salt
- 4 tbsp. unsalted butter
- 2 ½ cups flour
- 1 tbsp. sour cream to garnish for each serving

1. Directions:
   We will start by preparing the pierogi dough. For this, you need to whisk applesauce, vegetable oil, 1 tsp: kosher salt, one egg, and ½ cup of warm water in a bowl.
2. Take another bowl, put the flour in it, and gently stir in the mixture. On a floured surface, turn the dough out and knead it until smooth, dusting it with flour as required.
3. Now, cover and set it aside for half an hour.

BAKED CHICKEN REUBEN

Preparation Time: 20 minutes
Cooking Time: 90 minutes
Serving: 4

Ingredients:

- ¼ tsp. salt
- Six chicken breast halves
- 1/8 tsp. black pepper
- 1 16-oz. can sauerkraut
- 4 Swiss cheese slices
- 1 tbsp. chopped parsley

Directions:

1. Put the oven to 325 degrees Fahrenheit temperature to preheat.
2. Then, grease a baking dish and add chicken to it. Add salt and pepper to taste.
3. Over chicken, add sauerkraut and top it with slices of cheese. Then cover the dish with foil.
4. Bake in the oven for approx. 90 minutes till the chicken gets well cooked. Add chopped parsley and then serve.

COOKED VEGETABLE SALAD WITH MAYONNAISE

Preparation Time: 20 minutes
Cooking Time: 50 minutes
Serving: 4

Ingredients:

- Three peeled and chopped potatoes
- One peeled and chopped parsnip
- Three peeled and chopped carrots
- Four chopped gherkins
- Two peeled and chopped apples
- Five boiled eggs
- One squeeze of lemon juice
- One can of green peas
- 1 tsp. mustard

Directions:

1. Firstly, take a large saucepan and boil water in it. Now, cook the potatoes, carrots, and parsnip until they get soft.

2. Drain and then set it aside to let it cool.
3. After that, peel them, chop them into small cubes, and transfer them to a bowl.
4. Also, chop gherkins, eggs, and apples into little cubes.
5. Then add green peas, some lemon juice and season with salt and pepper.
6. Mix mayonnaise and mustard in another bowl and add it to the salad.

POLISH HONEY CAKE

Preparation Time: 20 minutes
Cooking Time: 50 minutes
Serving: 5

Ingredients:

- 1 tbsp. melted butter
- 2 cups fine dry bread crumbs
- ¼ cup brown sugar
- 1 cup honey and more for garnishing
- 1 cup whipped cream for garnishing
- Four separated eggs
- One toasted chopped hazelnut

Directions:

1. First, brush all the four brioche tins (1 ½ cup) that you can find at the bakery store with some butter that is melted beforehand, and a dash of brown sugar with bread crumbs (1 ¼ cup). Then set it aside.
2. Now preheat the oven to approximately 375 degrees F.
3. Put some honey into a medium-sized mixing bowl and pour a small-sized pot of boiling water over it. Warm it until the mixture gets loose. Now put the egg yolks and sugar into the honey, then beat until frothy.
4. Take the bowl off from the stove, and then you will need to whisk the rest of the hazelnuts and bread crumbs to combine.
5. Grab another bowl and start whisking the egg whites to become stiff, then fold the egg whites into the pre-made batter. Put the mixture in the prepared brioche tins and then bake for approximately 45 minutes.
6. When it cools down, remove the cake from the pan and top it with some whipped cream and add a sprinkle of honey.

RICE FLOUR CREPES

Cooking Time: 10 minutes

Preparation Time: 20 minutes
Serving: 4

Ingredients:

- Two eggs
- ¼ tsp. salt
- 1 cup milk
- 1 cup rice flour
- 1 tbsp. melted margarine

Directions:

1. First step is to add all the ingredients to a bowl. Beat them together and mix well till the mixture gets smooth.
2. Pour the mixture in a skillet with the help of ¼ cup measure and make sure that the skillet is greased and hot.
3. Now, turn the skillet to uniformly distributed batter.
4. Take care to cook about 35 seconds per side.

POLISH PASTA AND POTATOES

Cooking Time: 10 minutes

Preparation Time: 20 minutes
Serving: 4

Ingredients:

- Four potatoes, cut into cubes
- One chopped onion
- Two green bell peppers
- ½ tsp. onion powder
- ½ tsp. salt
- ¼ tsp. black pepper

- ¼ cup vegetable oil
- Four pasta servings

Directions:

1. Firstly cook pasta in a big pot of boiling salted water.
2. Now put butter or margarine in a skillet over medium heat.
3. Sauté cabbage and onions until they become tender.
4. Drain the pasta, and return to the pot. Put cabbage and onion mixture to the noodles, and then toss.
5. In the end, season it with salt and pepper to taste.

POLISH VEGETARIAN CABBAGE ROLLS

Preparation Time: 20 minutes
Cooking Time: 50 minutes
Serving: 4

Ingredients:

One large, fresh cabbage

Ingredients for the Filling:

- 2 cups of cooked brown rice
- 1 pound of Veggie Crumbles
- ½ cup of onion, minced
- One clove of garlic, minced
- 1 tsp. ground ginger
- 1 tbsp. sweet paprika
- 1 tbsp. parsley, roughly chopped
- 1 tsp. black pepper
- Two large eggs
- ½ cup of vegetable broth
- 2 tbsp. extra virgin olive oil
- Ingredients for the Sauce:
- 1 12 ounces can have diced tomatoes
- 1 12 ounces can have tomato soup

Directions:

1. First, core the cabbage and place it into a large pot filled with water. Set over medium heat and bring to a boil. Once boiling, reduce the heat and cover. Cook for 10 minutes or until soft. Remove after this time and let it set to cool.
2. While the cabbage is cooking, use a separate large pot and set over medium heat. Add in the olive oil. Once the oil is hot, add in the onions and garlic. Cook them for 3 to 5 minutes or until translucent. Then add the Veggie

Crumbles, cooked brown rice, minced onion, minced garlic, ground ginger, sweet paprika, chopped parsley, and black pepper. Stir to mix.

3. Separate the cabbage into six large leaves. Then preheat the oven to 375 degrees F.
4. Divide the filling into six parts and fill the cabbage leaves. Wrap the leaves around the contents and set them in a baking dish, end side down..
5. Use a medium bowl and add the tomato soup and diced tomatoes. Stir to mix. Fill half of the diced tomato can with water and add to the sauce. Stir again. Spoon this sauce over the rolls and cover it with a sheet of aluminum foil.
6. Place into the preheated oven to bake for 45 minutes or until tender. Take from the oven and set aside for 5 minutes before dishing.

POLISH MEAT PATTIES

Cooking Time: 15 minutes

Preparation Time: 25 minutes
Serving: 4

Ingredients:

- Chopped garlic, two teaspoons
- Chopped red onions, three tablespoons
- Chopped cilantro, half cup
- Minced beef meat, two cups
- Chopped fresh dill, two tablespoons
- Vegetable oil, two tablespoons
- Salt to taste
- Minced turkey meat, two cups
- Black pepper to taste
- Eggs, two
- All-purpose flour, two tablespoons
- Butter, two teaspoons

Directions:

1. Add the onions and the garlic to a large bowl.
2. Add in the rest of the ingredients.
3. Make round patties from the mixture.
4. Heat the oil and butter in a pan.
5. Fry the meat patties.
6. Dish the patties out when the patties turn golden brown on both sides.
7. Add cilantro on top.
8. You can serve it with any sauce that you prefer.
9. The dish is ready to be served.

POLISH STUFFED LOIN

Cooking Time: 20 minutes

Preparation Time: 30 minutes
Serving: 4

Ingredients:

- Golden apples, one can
- Bread crumbs, two cups
- Minced garlic, one teaspoon
- Orange zest, one teaspoon
- Dried cranberries, half cup
- Sour cream, one cup
- Pork loins, two pounds
- Dry white wine, one cup
- Dried thyme, one tablespoon
- Unsalted butter, one tablespoon
- Cilantro, a quarter cup
- Ground cloves, half teaspoon
- Crushed black pepper to taste
- Salt, to taste

Directions:

1. Take a small pan.
2. Add the butter.
3. Add the garlic into the pan.
4. Add the sliced apples and sour cream into the pan.
5. Add the dried cranberries and orange zest into the pan.
6. Add the bread crumbs and cook the ingredients well.
7. Add the stuffing into the pork loins and add the spices on top of the loins.
8. Roast the loins for fifteen to twenty minutes.
9. Add the cilantro on top before serving.
10. Your dish is ready to be served.

POLISH BEEF SIRLOIN

Preparation Time: 10 minutes
Cooking Time: 20 minutes
Serving: 4

Ingredients:

- Garlic, one tablespoon
- Bay leaves, one
- Allspice powder, two teaspoons
- Black pepper, one tablespoon
- Dried marjoram, one tablespoon
- Dried chilies, eight
- Beef sirloin, one pound
- Chopped red onion, half cup
- Passata paste, one cup
- Vegetable oil, two tablespoons
- Chopped cilantro leaves to garnish

- Salt, to taste

Directions:

1. Take a large pan.
2. In the pan, combine the oil and onions.
3. Cook till the onions are tender and transparent.
4. Add the garlic into the pan.
5. Cook the mixture well.
6. Add the passata paste and spices.
7. Cook the mixture for five minutes.
8. Add the beef sirloin into the pan.
9. Cook the ingredients well.
10. Add the rest of the ingredients.
11. Cook for 10 minutes with the lid on.
12. Decorate with cilantro leaves, if desired.
13. Your dish is ready to be served.

POLISH CHEESE AND BACON PIEROGI

Preparation Time: 30 minutes
Cooking Time: 30 minutes
Serving: 4

Ingredients:

- Salt
- Black pepper, to taste
- Dumpling dough, one pack
- Sour cream, one cup
- Chopped chives, one cup
- Chopped bacon, one cup
- Mozzarella cheese, half cup
- Minced garlic, two tablespoons
- Horseradish, two tablespoons
- Chopped parsley, half cup
- Olive oil, two tablespoons

Directions:

1. Take a large bowl.
2. Add the sour cream to it.
3. Beat the ingredients until they turn fluffy.
4. Add the chopped bacon, mozzarella cheese, minced garlic, and grated horseradish.
5. Mix all the ingredients well.
6. Season the mixture with salt and pepper.
7. Roll out the dumpling dough.
8. Cut circles and add the mixture into the dough.
9. Close the dumplings.

10. Add the dumplings into a large saucepan full of boiling water.
11. Cook the pierogi for five minutes and then drain it out.
12. Fry the dumplings in olive oil until they turn golden brown on both sides.
13. Dish out the pierogi and garnish it with chopped parsley leaves.
14. Your dish is ready to be served.

POLISH BEEF GOULASH

Preparation Time: 10 minutes
Cooking Time: 20 minutes
Serving: 4

Ingredients:

- Garlic, one tablespoon
- Bay leaves, one
- Allspice powder, two teaspoons
- Black pepper, one tablespoon
- Bell pepper, one cup
- All-purpose flour, three tablespoons
- Tomato paste, half cup
- Dry red wine, half cup
- Chopped red onion, half cup
- Ground beef, one pound
- Coldwater, one cup
- Beef broth, half cup
- Vegetable oil, two tablespoons
- Chopped cilantro leaves to garnish
- Salt, to taste

Directions:

1. Take a large pan.
2. In the pan, combine the oil and onions.
3. Cook until the onions are tender and transparent.
4. Add the garlic into the pan.
5. Cook the mixture well.
6. Add the tomato paste and spices.
7. Cook the mixture for five minutes.
8. Add the cooked red wine and beef broth into the pan.
9. Cook the ingredients well.
10. Add the flour, bell peppers, ground beef, and cold water.
11. Cover the pan and cook for 10 minutes.
12. Garnish the dish with chopped cilantro leaves.
13. Your dish is ready to be served.

POLISH SAUSAGE AND CABBAGE SOUP

Preparation Time: 20 minutes
Cooking Time: 10-12 hours
Serving: 5

Ingredients:

- 4 cups cabbage
- Two peeled and chopped carrots
- 2 cups caraway seeds
- Two peeled and chopped potatoes
- One peeled and chopped onion
- 4 cups chicken broth
- 1 lb. Polish sausage

Directions:

1. Firstly, add the first five listed ingredients into a slow cooker.
2. Then pour the chicken broth, cover it, and cook for 10-12 hours on low heat.
3. Flavor with salt and pepper to taste.
4. Serve.

POLISH PASTA AND CABBAGE

Preparation Time: 20 minutes
Cooking Time: 50 minutes
Serving: 4

Ingredients:

- ½ cup yellow onion
- 4 cups cabbages
- Eight oz. farfalle pasta
- ¼ cup butter
- Salt and pepper to taste
- 1 tsp. caraway seed
- ½ cup sour cream

Directions:

1. Firstly, take a big skillet and melt some butter overheat in it.
2. Now sauté the onion till it gets transparent.
3. Then combine cabbage and sauté for about 5 minutes till it gets tender.
4. Add caraway seeds, salt, and pepper and stir.
5. Side by side, take salted water and cook noodles the same way as written on the package. Take care not to overcook and drain it well.
6. Finally, stir noodles into the cabbage, onions, and sour cream.
7. Continue stirring it and cook for five more minutes.

POLISH GNOCCHI

Preparation Time: 20 minutes
Cooking Time: 10 minutes
Serving: 4

Ingredients:

- Six russet potatoes, boiled and mashed
- 1 cup of ricotta cheese
- Two large eggs
- 1 to 2 cups of all-purpose flour
- Pinch of salt
- 2 tbsp. melted butter

Directions:

1. Use a large bowl and add in the mashed potatoes, ricotta cheese, and large eggs. Stir until smooth inconsistency.
2. Then add in one cup of flour. Mix well and, if the dough is still sticky, add another cup of flour.
3. Roll the dough until at least 1 centimeter in length. Cut this dough into small, even-sized pieces.
4. Fill a large pot with water and set over medium heat. Season the water with a touch of salt. Once the water is boiling, gently drop in the gnocchi. Boil for 2 minutes or until they begin to float to the surface.
5. Allow them to sit for 1 to 2 minutes before serving with melted butter.

POLISH APPLE PIE

Preparation Time: 20 minutes
Cooking Time: 50 minutes
Serving: 5

Ingredients for the Crust:

- 4 cups of all-purpose flour
- ½ cup of white sugar
- 2 tsp. baking powder
- 1 cup of soft salted butter
- Four large eggs
- 1 tsp. pure vanilla extract
- 3 tbsp. whole milk

Ingredients for the Filling:

- 2 pounds of Gala apples, peeled, cored, and thinly sliced
- 2 pounds of Red Delicious apples, peeled, cored, and thinly sliced
- 2 tsp. ground cinnamon

Directions:

1. First, make the crust. For this, preheating your oven to 350 degrees F.

2. While the oven is heating up, use a large bowl and add all-purpose flour, white sugar, and baking powder. Stir to mix evenly.
3. Add the butter and cut in with a pastry cutter until coarse. Then add in the eggs and pure vanilla. Mix everything until moist.
4. Add in the whole milk and mix until a sticky dough begins to form. Transfer the dough to a lightly floured surface. Knead for 1-2 minutes or until the dough sticks together.
5. Divide the dough into two pieces. Make sure one piece is at least ⅔ of the dough, and the other is ⅓ of the dough. Wrap the smaller dough in a sheet of plastic wrap. Place into the freezer for 30 minutes. Place the larger piece of dough into a 9-inch springform pan.
6. Place the dough in the springform pan into the oven to bake for 5 minutes or until golden around the edges. Remove from the oven and set on a wire rack to cool.
7. Meanwhile, make the filling. To do this, add the Gala and Red Delicious apples into a large pot. Add in the ground cinnamon and cook over medium heat for 5 to 7 minutes or until the soft apples. Remove from the heat.
8. Spread the filling into the cooked crust.
9. Then, take the small portion of dough out of the freezer. Use a cheese grater and grate it over the filling.
10. Place into the oven to bake for 40 to 45 minutes or until the top is golden in color. Remove from the oven and place on a wire rack to cool thoroughly before serving.

HERRING IN CREAM

Preparation time: 10 minutes

Cooking time: 0 minutes

Servings: 4

Ingredients

- Four herring fillets, skinned
- 3 Tablespoons of vinegar
- One apple
- ½ sweet onion
- Two allspice berries or 1/16 teaspoon ground allspice
- One bay leaf
- One teaspoon cinnamon
- 1 cup thick sour cream
- 1 Tablespoon brown mustard
- Two teaspoons powdered sugar
- Thinly sliced onion for garnish
- Parsley for garnish

Directions

1. If the herring hasn't already been soaked, place the herring fillets into a bowl of cold water in the refrigerator for a day. Change the water to freshwater every 6 to 8 hours.
2. Dry the herring with paper towels.
3. Cut the herring into 1-inch to 1 ½ inch pieces.
4. Put the herring pieces into a glass or ceramic bowl.
5. Pour the vinegar over the herring.
6. Peel the apple and grate over the herring in the bowl.
7. Peel the onion and dice it into cubes. Add the onion to the bowl.

8. Add the allspice, bay leaf, and cinnamon to the bowl
9. Blend the sour cream, mustard, and powdered sugar in a separate bowl until the mixture is smooth.
10. Pour the sour cream mixture over the herring, apples, and onions. Make sure the cream covers each herring fillet.
11. Cover and refrigerate upto 3 hours before serving.
12. Serve with the onion slices and parsley

ROLLMOPS

Preparation time: 10 minutes

Cooking time: 30 minutes

Servings: 4

Ingredients for Rollmops

- Eight salt herring fillets with skin
- Water for soaking herring
- Polish mustard or other brown mustard
- Black pepper
- One onion
- Two dill pickles
- Marinade Ingredients
- 2 cups of water
- 1 cup of white vinegar
- Six teaspoons sugar
- Two bay leaves
- Four allspice berries
- Five peppercorns
- One teaspoon mustard seed
- 2 Tablespoons vegetable oil
- Three onions
- Salt

Directions:

1. Soak Herring
2. If the herring is fresh and has not been soaked, put the herring fillets in a pan of water for 24 hours. Change the water every 6 to 8 hours.
3. Transfer the fillets to a plate and pat them dry with paper towels. Cover with plastic cling wrap and refrigerate.
4. Prepare the Rollmops
5. Finely chop the one onion.
6. Cut the dill pickles into quarters so that you have eight pieces.
7. Remove the herring fillets from the refrigerator.
8. Take each herring fillet:
9. Spread the fillet with brown mustard.
10. Sprinkle some pepper over the mustard.
11. Spread chopped onion on top of the mustard
12. Place a pickle quarter at the smaller end of the fillet and roll up. Secure with a toothpick.

13. Put the rollmops into a sterilized, wide mouth, glass canning jar.
14. When all of the fillets have been rolled and put into the jar, cap the jar and put it into the refrigerator.
15. Prepare the Marinade
16. Pour water, vinegar, and sugar into a pot.
17. Add the bay leaves, allspice, peppercorns, mustard seed, and vegetable oil to the pot.
18. Add salt to taste.
19. Bring the marinade to a boil.
20. Finely chop the three onions. Add the chopped onion to the boiling marinade and boil for two more minutes.
21. Take the pot off the burner and cool until it is warm.
22. Pickle the Rollmops
23. Remove the rollmops from the refrigerator and uncap the jar.
24. Pour as much of the warm marinade into the jar of rollmops as will fit.
25. Tightly cap the jar.
26. Turn the jar upside down and right side up several times to distribute the marinade. (Don't shake the jar).
27. Refrigerate for five days.
28. Serve Rollmops
29. Arrange the rollmops on a serving platter and drizzle them with little reserved pickling juices.
30. Garnish with chopped, fresh dill.
31. I serve rollmops at weekend family dinners as a cold, plated appetizer (zakuski).

PICKLED CARROTS

Preparation time: 10 minutes

Cooking time: 40 minutes

Servings: 4

Ingredients

- 10 cups of bottled or filtered water
- 2 cups distilled white vinegar
- Two teaspoons pickling salt
- 1/2 cup sugar
- Six cloves garlic
- 2 Tablespoon fresh dill, chopped
- 46 peppercorns, divided
- 2 pounds small baby carrots
- One large onion, peeled and sliced thinly
- Six teaspoons celery seeds
- 12 teaspoons mustard seeds
- Equipment
- 5 to 6 sterilized canning jars (1-pint) with lids and rings

Directions

1. Put the water, vinegar, salt, and sugar into a large non-reactive pot. Bring to a boil.

2. Add the garlic, dill, 16 peppercorns, carrots, and onion to the pot. Reduce heat and simmer for 10 minutes. You want the carrots to be crisp and not soft. Remove from burner.
3. In the bottom of each sterilized jar, place six peppercorns, two teaspoons of mustard seeds, and one teaspoon of celery seeds.
4. Use a slotted spoon, transfer the carrots and onions to each jar. Pack the carrots and onions, leaving 1/2 inch to 1-inch at the top.
5. Return the pot with the marinade to the burner and bring it to a boil.
6. Carefully spoon the marinade over the carrots and onions in each jar. Leave at least 1/2 inch of headspace at the top of each jar.
7. Wipe the rims of the jars with a wet paper towel to remove any marinade that may have splashed.
8. Tightly seal each jar with a lid and ring. Turn the jars upside down to cool. After the jars have cooled, turn them right side up.
9. Store in the refrigerator. I wait five days before serving the pickled carrots. I tried to use all of the carrots four weeks from the day they were pickled.
10. Notes
11. Instead of whole baby carrots, you can also use 2 pounds of shredded carrots or 2 pounds of peeled carrot strips in this recipe.

EGG SALAD

Preparation time: 10 minutes

Cooking time: 20 minutes

Servings: 4

Ingredients

- Six eggs
- ¼ cup of finely chopped onions
- ¼ cup of finely chopped celery
- ¼ chopped parsley
- ¼ cup chopped chives
- 2 Tablespoons pickled cucumbers, cubed
- Two peeled apples, grated and sprinkled with lemon juice for garnish

Directions

1. Prepare the Salad
2. Boil the eggs
3. Cool the eggs and cut them into small cubes. Add to a large bowl
4. Add the onions, celery, parsley, chives, pickled cucumber.
5. Mix well
6. Add dressing (see below) and toss to mix
7. Sprinkle the grated apples over the top
8. Dressing Use ONE of these dressings or use the dressing of your choice.
9. ½ cup to 1 cup Horseradish Sauce
10. ½ cup to 1 cup Basic Mayo – Sour Cream Sauce
11. ½ cup to 1 cup plain mayonnaise

Preparation time: 10 minutes

Cooking time: 20 minutes

Servings: 4

Ingredients

- Six medium potatoes
- Eight large carrots
- Six large pickled cucumbers
- One large dill pickle
- One medium onion
- One large apple
- Three cans (8.5 ounces each) peas, drained
- One can (8.5 ounces) sweet corn, drained
- Eight eggs, hard-boiled
- Salt and pepper to taste
- ½ cup mayonnaise
- ½ cup plain yogurt

Directions

1. Wash the vegetables.
2. Cook the potatoes in a pan of water until they are tender.
3. Remove the potatoes from the water and allow them to cool.
4. Cook the carrots in a pan of water until they are tender.
5. Remove the carrots from the water and allow them to cool.
6. Peel the potatoes and carrots.
7. Finely dice the potatoes. Add them to a large bowl.
8. Finely dice the carrots. Add them to the bowl.
9. Peel the cucumbers, dice them, and add to the bowl.
10. Peel the dill pickle, dice it, and add to the bowl.
11. Finely chop the onion and add to the bowl.
12. Peel and core the apple. Dice the apple and add to the bowl.
13. Add the drained peas to the bowl.
14. Add the drained corn and add to the bowl.
15. Peel the hard-boiled eggs.
16. Finely chop the eggs and put them into the bowl.
17. Add salt and pepper to taste.
18. Toss the ingredients to mix them.
19. Add one cup of Basic Mayonnaise Sauce and toss to coat the ingredients. You can add more of the sauce if you'd like.

Notes

You can use any dressing you like with this salad. Two other dressings I have used that are milder:

- ½ cup of mayonnaise and ½ cup of sour cream mixture.
- ½ cup of mayonnaise and ½ cup of plain yogurt mixed.

POTATO SALAD

Preparation time: 10 minutes

Cooking time: 20 minutes

Servings: 4

Ingredients

- Six large potatoes
- Four eggs
- 2 Dill pickles
- ½ large white onion
- 3 Tablespoons of fresh parsley, chopped
- 3 Tablespoons of fresh dill, chopped
- Salt and pepper to taste

Directions

1. Wash and scrub the potatoes.
2. Boil the unpeeled potatoes till tender in salted water. (20 to 30 minutes).
3. Drain and cool the potatoes.
4. Boil the eggs until hard-boiled.
5. Cool the eggs.
6. Peel and slice the potatoes into tiny pieces.
7. Peel the eggs and dice them.
8. Chop the Dill pickles
9. Chop the onions.

10. Add the potatoes, eggs, pickles, and onions to a large bowl.
11. Add the parsley and dill.
12. Add salt and pepper to taste.
13. Toss the ingredients until they're mixed
14. Add the dressing (See below).

Dressing Use ONE of these dressings or use the dressing of your choice.

- ½ to ¾ cup of plain mayonnaise
- ½ to ¾ cup Basic Mayo-Sour Cream Sauce **
- ½ to ¾ cup Lemon Garlic Chive Sauce **

BASIC MAYONNAISE SAUCE

Preparation time: 10 minutes

Cooking time: 0 minutes

Servings: 4

Ingredients

- 1 ½ cups mayonnaise
- 1 cup sour cream
- 3 Tablespoons brown mustard
- 1 ½ teaspoon lemon juice
- Two teaspoons powdered sugar
- Salt to taste
- Pepper to taste

Directions

1. Add all the ingredients to a medium mixing bowl.
2. Blend well with a hand mixer.
3. Cover the bowl with plastic wrap.
4. Refrigerate for upto 1 hour and then use.

HORSERADISH SAUCE

Preparation time: 10 minutes

Cooking time: 0 minutes

Servings: 4

Ingredients

- 2/3 cup sour cream
- 2/3 cup mayonnaise
- 2 Tablespoons prepared horseradish

- Juice of 1 lemon
- Four teaspoons powdered sugar

Directions

1. Add all ingredients to a medium mixing bowl.
2. Blend all the ingredients using a hand mixer.
3. Cover the bowl with plastic wrap.
4. Refrigerate for at least 1 hour and then use.

LEMON GARLIC CHIVE SAUCE

Preparation time: 10 minutes

Cooking time: 0 minutes

Servings: 4

Ingredients

- 1-1/2 cups sour cream
- Two garlic cloves, minced
- 2 Tablespoons chopped fresh chives
- 1-1/2 teaspoons lemon zest
- 3 Tablespoons fresh lemon juice
- Salt to taste
- Pepper to taste

Directions

1. Add all ingredients to a medium mixing bowl.
2. Blend with a hand mixer.
3. Cover the bowl with plastic wrap.
4. Cool for at least 1 hour in the refrigerator before using.

Notes

- You can substitute mayonnaise for the sour cream
- You can skip the garlic if you'd like

BACON AND SAUSAGE APPETIZER

Preparation time: 10 minutes

Cooking time: 40 minutes

Servings: 4

Ingredients

- 2 pounds thick-cut smoked bacon, sliced
- 2 pounds smoked kielbasa

- 1 cup brown sugar

Directions

1. Cut each bacon slice in half at the midpoint.
2. Cut the kielbasa into 1-inch-wide pieces.
3. For each piece of kielbasa:
4. Wrap one bacon strip around a piece of kielbasa.
5. Secure the bacon with a toothpick.
6. Set aside on a plate.
7. Continue until all of the kielbasa pieces are wrapped in bacon.
8. Preheat the oven to 350º F.
9. Line a rimmed baking sheet with tinfoil (for easier cleanup).
10. Place a cooling rack or grate on the baking sheet. This will allow bacon drippings to go into the pan underneath.
11. Place the bacon-wrapped kielbasa pieces on top of the rack.
12. Sprinkle brown sugar over the bacon-wrapped kielbasa pieces.
13. Bake at 350º F for 30 to 35 minutes. You want the bacon nice and crispy.
14. Transfer the bacon-wrapped kielbasa pieces to paper towels to drain off any remaining bacon grease.
15. Serve hot. You can eat them like they are or with brown mustard or honey mustard for dipping.

HOT PRUNE & BACON ROLL-UPS

Preparation time: 10 minutes

Cooking time: 30 minutes

Servings: 4

Ingredients

- 24 four-inch slices of thin bacon
- 24 dried prunes, pitted
- 24 blanched almonds

Directions

1. Preheat the oven to 375ºF.
2. Soak the prunes in water for 10 minutes.
3. For each prune:
4. Slide a blanched almond into the hole in the prune where the pit was removed.
5. Tightly roll a strip of bacon around the prune. Secure with a toothpick.
6. Repeat this for all of the prunes.
7. Line 2 rimmed baking sheets with tinfoil (for easier cleanup).
8. Divide the rolled prunes between the two baking dishes.
9. Move the baking dishes in the oven and bake for 15 minutes.
10. Flip the roll-ups over and bake for 5 to 10 more minutes. The bacon should be nice and crispy.
11. Serve the roll-ups hot from the oven.

Notes

- You can substitute whole, dried, pitted plums in this recipe. Fresh plums do not work well.
- Since different ovens heat differently at the same temperature, keep an eye on the roll-ups after the first 15 minutes of cooking time. The bacon should be crispy but not burned.

HOT PRUNE, CHEESE, & BACON ROLL-UPS

Preparation time: 10 minutes

Cooking time: 40 minutes

Servings: 4

Ingredients

- 24 four-inch slices of thin bacon
- 24 dried prunes, pitted
- One package of cream cheese, 8 ounces, at room temperature

Directions

1. Preheat the oven to 375º F.
2. Soak the prunes in water for 10 minutes.
3. Put the softened cream cheese into an icing bag.
4. For each prune:
5. Fill the prune with cream cheese, using the hole in the center of the prune where the pit was removed.
6. Tightly roll a strip of bacon around the prune. Secure with a toothpick.
7. Repeat this for all of the prunes.
8. Divide the rolled prunes between two large baking dishes.
9. Put the baking dishes in the oven and bake for 15 minutes.
10. Flip the roll-ups over and bake for 5 to 10 more minutes. The bacon should be nice and crispy.
11. Serve the roll-ups hot from the oven.

Notes

- Since different ovens heat differently at the same temperature, keep an eye on the roll-ups after the first 15 minutes of cooking time. You want the bacon to be crispy and not burnt.
- You can serve these roll-ups plain or with a dipping sauce.

Preparation time: 10 minutes

Cooking time: 50 minutes

Servings: 4

Ingredients

- 24 extra-large white mushrooms, washed
- 4 Tablespoons unsalted butter
- One large onion, minced
- One clove garlic, peeled and minced
- ½ red pepper, finely chopped
- 6 Tablespoons boiled ham, diced
- 2 Tablespoons fresh parsley, chopped
- 4 Tablespoons bread crumbs
- 2 ounces Mozzarella cheese, grated
- Two eggs
- Salt and pepper to taste

Directions

1. For each mushroom, cut the stem off at the base of the cap. Set the stems aside.
2. Finely chop the mushroom stems.
3. Sauté the mushroom stems, minced onion, garlic, and chopped red pepper together in butter. You want the onions to be translucent.
4. Add the boiled ham to the mushroom stems and onions. Stir. Simmer for 5 minutes. Add the fresh, chopped parsley and stir. Remove from the burner and cool.
5. After the stuffing mixture has completely cooled, add the bread crumbs, mozzarella cheese, eggs, salt, and pepper. Mix well.
6. Preheat oven to 350º F.
7. Press the bottom of each mushroom cap so that there's an indentation. Fill each mushroom cap with the filling mixture. A mound of filling works well.
8. Put the stuffed mushrooms in a baking dish.
9. Cook in the preheated oven for 20 to 30 minutes.
10. Serve hot.

GLAZED CARROTS

Preparation time: 10min
Cooking time: 25min

Servings: 6-8

Ingredients:

- Two batches carrots, cleansed (small)
- 2-3 tbsp. oil
- 1 tsp. Black pepper
- 1 tsp. Sea salt
- 1 tbsp. Honey
- 2 tbsp. fresh Dill, chopped

Directions:

1. First, preheat the oven, 400F.
2. Clean the carrots and slice them in half.
3. In a baking pan, place all ingredients and toss to coat the carrots evenly.
4. Cook 25 minutes in the oven.
5. Once done, sprinkle with dill.
6. Serve and enjoy!

PICKLED CUCUMBERS

Preparation time: 10 minutes

Cooking time: 30 minutes

Servings: 4

Ingredients

- 2-quart canning jar with lid, sterilized
- 20 pickling cucumbers (4-6 inches long), washed and dried
- Two fresh horseradish root pieces, each 6-inches long
- Four teaspoons mustard seeds
- Fourier cloves peeled garlic, diced
- Four stems of dried dill, with flower and seeds
- Ten peppercorns
- Six allspice berries or ¼ to ½ teaspoon ground allspice
- Two bay leaves
- Cherry, grape, or black currant leaf (optional)
- 2 quarts bottled or filtered water
- 4 Tablespoons pickling salt or kosher salt

Directions

1. Wash the cucumbers and then soak them in cold water for 3 to 4 hours.
2. Peel the horseradish root and slice it into 4 to 6-inch strips.
3. Place the following ingredients in the bottom of the jar:
4. ½ of the sliced horseradish
5. Two teaspoons mustard seeds,
6. ½ of the diced garlic,
7. ½ of the dried dill,
8. Five peppercorns
9. ½ of the allspice (berries or ground)
10. One bay leaf cherry, grape, or black currant leaf (if used) Note: Only use one and not all three in a single batch.
11. Tightly pack the cucumbers upright into the sterile jar.
12. Add the remaining sliced horseradish, mustard seeds, diced garlic, dill, peppercorns, allspice, bay leaf, and optional cherry, grape, or black currant leaf between and around the cucumbers.
13. Place some cucumbers horizontally at the top of the jar and press down. You want to prevent the cucumbers from bobbing up when adding the brine.
14. Start by 2 quarts of water to a boil.
15. Add the salt and stir.
16. Take the pot off the burner and allow the water to cool until it's warm.
17. Fill the jar of pickles with the saltwater to within ¼ inch from the top
18. If you're using a wide-mouth jar or container and any cucumbers are floating to the top, place a small, sterilized ceramic plate or cup on top of the cucumbers to keep them submerged.
19. Clean the rims of the jars with a wet paper towel to remove any marinade that may have splashed.
20. Loosely cap the jar with the sterile lid. The mixture will ferment, and you need to allow the gases to escape.
21. An alternative is to cover the jar opening with cheesecloth and secure it with a large rubber band. This is a good Direction for a wide-mouth jar or container.
22. Some brine will probably seep out of the loosened cap, so place the jar on a tray or counter at room temperature (50º F to 60º F). If you have a cool, dark pantry, that would be ideal.
23. After a few days, the brine will become cloudy, which is normal.
24. Allow the cucumbers to ferment from 1 to 3 weeks. Taste test during that time. Tighten the lid and move the jar to the refrigerator when you like the taste.

Notes

- Make sure to use pickling cucumbers and not regular cucumbers. The taste and consistency are much better.
- Some cooks like to cut off the tips of each cucumber before pickling.
- You don't want cucumbers to float up and touch the cap because this can result in mold.
- Some cooks prefer to add hot brine to the jar of cucumbers. I think this often "cooks" the cucumbers and produces a softer cucumber pickle. I like to cool the brine until it's warm and not hot. This results in a crispier spot.
- Instead of packing the jar with whole pickles, you can cut them in halves or quarters. You can also slice each cucumber into round pieces. Whatever option you pick, ensure that the cucumbers can't float up to the cap once you add the brine. Place two or more whole cucumbers horizontally on top of the sliced cucumbers to block floating.
- You can experiment with adding one of the following leaves to a batch: grape, cherry, raspberry, black currant, oak, or mustard.

COTTAGE CHEESE DIP

Preparation time: 5 minutes

Cooking time: 5 minutes

Servings: 1

Ingredients

- 1 cup cottage cheese
- Six radishes
- One bunch of chives (1/2 cup finely chopped)
- One heaped tablespoon of Greek yogurt
- Salt pepper

Directions

1. Add cottage cheese to a bowl.
2. Finely chop the radishes and chives and add to the cottage cheese.
3. Add Greek yogurt.
4. Season with salt and pepper.
5. Mix everything with the fork.
6. Serve on bread or with boiled potatoes.

SALMON SPREAD

Preparation time: 10 minutes

Cooking time: 30 minutes

Servings: 1

Ingredients

- 7 ounces piece salmon
- Two cloves garlic
- Two tablespoons ketchup
- One teaspoon chopped onion
- One teaspoon butter
- 4 ounces cream cheese
- One teaspoon fresh dill

Directions

Sprinkle the raw fish with salt and pepper and fry in butter for 8-11 minutes or until done.Take out the cooked fish from the pan and let it cool. Once the fish is cold, put it in a blender or food processor with ketchup, cream cheese, and garlic and blend into a smooth paste. Remove from blender to a bowl and add the finely chopped onion and dill. Mix with a spoon or spatula. Add salt and pepper to taste and Cool it before serving.

SMOKED SALMON DIP

Preparation time: 10 minutes

Cooking time: 0 minutes

Servings: 5

Ingredients:

- 1/2 cup sour cream
- 8 ounces cream cheese, softened at room temperature
- Two lemons
- 1/8 teaspoon black pepper
- 8 ounces smoked salmon, finely chopped
- Three tablespoons chopped chives, plus more for garnish
- One tablespoon Dijon mustard
- Two tablespoons small capers
- 1/2 teaspoon pepper

Directions

In the stand mixer bowl, beat the cream cheese and sour cream with the paddle attachment on medium speed until smooth. Add the chives, mustard, capers, zest, and juice of 1 lemon and black pepper with the mixer on low. Mix until all ingredients are incorporated. Transfer to a bowl and whisk the mixture into a smooth mixture.

Fold in the salmon and pepper, if using, by hand. Taste and add the juice of the remaining lemon, one teaspoon at a time, if you think it is necessary. Serve immediately or refrigerate until serving.

FISH PASTE WITH CHILI

Preparation time: 10 minutes

Cooking time: 10 minutes

Servings: 2

Ingredients

- 6 ounces smoked mackerel
- One pinch chili
- Two tablespoons olive oil
- 3 ounces cream cheese
- Two teaspoons lemon juice
- Two tablespoons tablespoon horseradish

Directions

Carefully peel the skin from the mackerel and remove the bones. Put all ingredients in a blender and mix briefly until well blended. Serve.

POLISH GARLIC SAUCE

Preparation time: 15 minutes

Cooking time: 15 minutes

Servings: 1

Ingredients

- Four garlic cloves, finely chopped
- 1/2 cup yogurt
- 1/2 cup mayonnaise
- 1/2 teaspoon salt
- 1/4 teaspoon pepper
- One teaspoon parsley or thyme chopped, fresh or dried

Directions

Combine all ingredients; allow to rest for 13-15 minutes to allow the flavors to merge before serving. Mix well and serve.

BOHEMIAN KOLACHES

Preparation time: 30 minutes

Cooking time: 10 minutes

Servings: 3

Ingredients

- Two packages (1/4 ounce each) active dry yeast
- 1/2 cup sugar, divided
- 2 cups warm milk
- 6 1/2 cups all-purpose flour
- Four egg yolks, room temperature
- One teaspoon salt
- 1/4 cup butter, softened
- 2 cups canned plums, poppy seed, cherry filling
- One egg white, beaten

Directions

1. Mix yeast and one tablespoon of sugar in warm milk in a bowl. Let alone for 12 minutes. In another bowl, stir 2 cups of flour, remaining sugar, egg yolks, salt, butter, and yeast/milk mixture. Mix until smooth. Add enough leftover flour to make a stiff dough.
2. Move the dough on a floured surface and knead for 7-10 minutes into a smooth and elastic dough. Add extra flour if necessary. Put dough in a Coated bowl and turn once to grease the top. Cover, let rise in a warm place until doubled in bulk, about 55-65 minutes.
3. Push the dough down and let it come up again. Roll out on a floured surface to 1/2-inch thickness. Cut with a tall glass or two ½-inch cutter. Place them on greased baking trays; let rise until doubled, about 43-46 minutes.
4. Press firmly in the center of each cake to make a hollow. Fill each cake with a heaped tablespoon of filling of your choice. Brush the dough with egg white. Bake at 355 F for 12-14 minutes or until the buns are lightly golden brown. Serve.

CAULIFLOWER GRANTEE

Preparation time: 10min
Cooking time: 40min

Servings: 4

Ingredients:

- 2 lb. Cauliflower florets, cook them al dente
- 2 cups of milk
- 2 tbsp. melted butter
- 2 tbsp. of Flour
- 1 Onion, chopped
- 1 tsp. Dijon mustard
- 1/8 tsp. thyme
- 1/8 tsp. Nutmeg
- ½ tsp. Black pepper
- 2 Garlic cloves, crushed
- 1/8 tsp. Cayenne
- Parmigiano-Reggiano cheese, grated

Directions:

1. Preheat oven, 375F.
2. Adjust on medium heat and place a saucepan. Add the butter/oil and onions. Cook for 5 minutes.
3. Now add the melted butter and the flour. Cook 2 minutes.
4. Add milk and all the other remaining ingredients. Once boiling, reduce the heat. Cook 2 minutes. Set aside.
5. Place the cauliflowers in a backing dish. Spoon the sauce over. Sprinkle with cheese. Bake for 30 minutes.
6. Serve sprinkled with parsley and enjoy!

PICKLED MUSHROOMS

Preparation time: 10 minutes

Cooking time: 30 minutes

Servings: 4

Ingredients

- 4 pounds fresh porcini mushrooms
- Water for the mushrooms
- One carrot, peeled and cut into strips
- 6 1-pint canning jars with lids and rings, sterilized
- Marinade
- 4 cups bottled or filtered water
- One large onion, chopped
- One garlic clove, peeled and chopped
- Two teaspoons white sugar
- One teaspoon pickling salt
- Six whole black peppercorns
- Three whole allspice berries or ½ teaspoon ground allspice
- One bay leaf
- One tablespoon prepared brown mustard
- 1 cup distilled white vinegar

Directions

1. Wash the mushrooms under running water. Trim the stems to remove dry parts. Cut the mushrooms into quarters or smaller pieces.
2. Put the mushrooms into a large saucepan or pot.
3. Add enough water to cover the mushrooms. Over medium heat, bring the water to a boil. Once the water boils, remove the saucepan or pot from the heat. Drain the water.
4. Put several carrot strips into each of your sterilized jars.
5. Pack each jar with the mushrooms so that the jars are ¾ filled.
6. Marinade
7. For the marinade, use a large, non-reactive saucepan.
8. To the saucepan, add the 3-1/2 cups water, chopped onion, chopped garlic, sugar, pickling sauce, peppercorns, allspice, bay leaf, and mustard. Stir the ingredients.
9. Using medium heat, bring the marinade to a boil. Once it boils, reduce the heat, and simmer gently for 15 minutes.

10. Add the vinegar to the simmering marinade. Stir and simmer for five more minutes. Remove the pot from the burner.
11. Pour the marinade evenly over mushrooms in the jars. Fill each jar to within 1/4 inch of the top.
12. Wipe the rims of the jars with a wet paper towel to remove any marinade that may have splashed.
13. Seal the jar tightly with the sterilized lid and ring. Turn the jars upside down and allow them to cool.
14. After they have cooled, turn each jar right side up.
15. Store the jars in the refrigerator for five days before eating. I tried to use all of the mushrooms four weeks from the day they were pickled.

Notes

- You can substitute three teaspoons of mustard seeds for the prepared brown mustard.

AIR FRYER RANCH KALE CHIPS

Preparation time: 2 minutes

Cooking time: 12 minutes

Servings: 5

Ingredients

- Ten kale leaves
- One teaspoon garlic powder
- One teaspoon onion powder
- One teaspoon dried dill
- Two tablespoons olive oil
- One tablespoon nutritional yeast flakes
- One teaspoon salt

Directions

Remove the curled leaves from the hard stalk of the kale. Break the leaves into smaller, bite-sized pieces. Beat the olive oil, nutritional yeast flakes, garlic powder, onion powder, dried dill, and salt in a large bowl. Add the pieces of kale to the bowl and toss. Make sure to cover the leaves with the herbs evenly. Add the kale to the air fryer basket. Set the air fryer to 410 F and cook for 12 minutes, shaking halfway through the cooking time. Serve.

KIELBASA APPETIZER WITH APPLE JELLY

Preparation time: 5 minutes

Cooking time: 2 hours

Servings: 15

Ingredients

- 2 pounds kielbasa
- 1 (18 ounces) jar of apple jelly

- 1 (9 ounces) jar of prepared mustard

Directions

Cut kielbasa 1/2-inch thick. Mix jelly and mustard in a slow cooker or crockpot. Add sliced kielbasa and mix until the meat is coated. Adjust the slow cooker on low to cook for 2 hours. Stir every 25-35 minutes. Serve.

RAW POLISH CARROT

Preparation time: 20 minutes

Cooking time: 0 minutes

Servings: 6

Ingredients

- Five large carrots, peeled and coarsely grated
- 1 Granny Smith apple, cored, peeled, and coarsely grated
- One tablespoon lemon juice
- One tablespoon sunflower oil
- 1/2 cup dark or light raisins, soaked in water for 15 minutes)
- Salt and sugar to taste

Directions

In a bowl, combine apple, lemon juice, carrots, sunflower or vegetable oil, drained raisins, salt to taste, and sugar to taste. After the ingredients are thoroughly mixed, cover and refrigerate until cold. Serve chilled.

POLISH PORK LARD SPREAD (SMALEC)

Preparation time: 20 minutes

Cooking time: 30 minutes

Servings: 2

Ingredients

- 2 1/4 pounds white pork fat or diced leaf lard
- Two onions, finely chopped
- Four cloves garlic, finely chopped
- 1/2-pound fat bacon, diced
- Two large sour apples, peeled, cored, and cut into small cubes
- 1/8 teaspoon pepper
- One teaspoon salt
- One teaspoon marjoram

Directions

Grind the diced white pork fat and put it in a large skillet. Sauté until fat is transparent, stirring occasionally. Add the onion, garlic, and bacon and fry until the bacon is golden brown and releases its fat. Add the apples and season with any marjoram, pepper, and salt to taste. Do not add too much salt since the bacon is probably quite salty. But you have to add enough to make the Smalec taste good.

Transfer to a stoneware jar or heat-resistant jar. Leave at room temperature until the fat has solidified. Serve this spread on rye bread topped with pickles.

POLISH PORK-AND-BEEF PATE

Preparation time: 100 minutes

Cooking time: 15 minutes

Servings: 5

Ingredients

- o   pounds beef, flank steak
- 1 pound of pork, boneless shoulder
- 11 ounces of pork fat
- One bay leaf
- Four allspice berries
- Five black peppercorns
- Two bread rolls, dry
- Two onions, peeled and thinly sliced
- Two tablespoons of vegetable oil
- Two teaspoons salt
- 1/4 teaspoon black pepper
- One pinch nutmeg
- Three cloves garlic, crushed
- One tablespoon vegetable oil
- One tablespoon breadcrumbs

Directions

Wash the beef, pork, and pork fat. Drain and transfer to a large saucepan. Add bay leaf, allspice, black peppercorns, and pour enough cold water to cover the meat. Simmer until the meat is cooked. Remove the pan from the heat. Place the buns on top of the stock to soak them. Sauté the peeled and thinly sliced onions in a bit of oil frying pan.

Grind the meat together with the roll and the fried onions twice in a meat grinder to a smooth consistency. Season with pepper, nutmeg, salt, and crushed garlic. Mix these ingredients well. The pâté mixture should be moist. If it is too dry, add some meat stock. When the meat has cooled, could you remove it from the stock?

Grease a mold or baking pan with oil and sprinkle with breadcrumbs. Transfer the pate mixture to the pan and fill it 3/4 full. Bake for about 45 minutes in an oven heated to 345 F. Allow to cool before removing, slicing, and serving.

CAULIFLOWER FRESH SALAD

Preparation time: 15min

Cooking time: 0 min

Servings: 6-8

Ingredients:

- 1 Cauliflower Head, medium
- 2 Dill pickles, chopped
- 1 Apple, peeled and seeded, chopped
- 4-5 basil leaves
- One can of corn, drained
- ½ cup of Mayo
- ¾ cup of Plain yogurt
- ½ tsp. Salt

Directions:

1. Dice the basil, apple, pickles, and cauliflower.
2. In a bowl, combine mayo, yogurt, and corn. Season with salt.
3. Now add diced veggies and stir to combine.
4. Chill before serving. Enjoy!

Note: Make sure to dice the veggies very, very small. This is the key!

SPRING CABBAGE WITH DILL

Preparation time: 10 minutes

Cooking time: 40 minutes

Servings: 4

Ingredients:

- One head cabbage, cored and shredded
- One bunch fresh dill, chopped
- 2 tbsps. unsalted butter
- 2 tsp. vegetable stock powder
- 2/3 cup water, or more to taste
- 1/4 cup sour cream
- salt and ground black pepper to taste

Directions:

In a pot, mix the vegetable stock powder, butter, dill, and cabbage, pour in water to cover. Let it simmer on low heat for about 30 minutes, stirring once in a while, until the cabbage becomes soft. Take off from the heat.

Mix the salt, sour cream, and 2 tbsps. of cooking liquid in a small bowl. Stir it into the cabbage mixture until well incorporated. Put pepper and salt to season.

BACON CAULIFLOWER SALAD

Preparation time: 15min
Cooking time: 10min

Servings: 4

Ingredients:

- 1 Cauliflower head
- 1 Iceberg lettuce, small, shredded
- One lb. cooked bacon, crumbled
- 2 tsp. Sugar
- ¼ cup Parmesan cheese, grated
- 1 cup of Mayo

Directions:

1. First, remove the green leaves out of the cauliflower. Break it into flowerets and wash.
2. Layer the cauliflower in a bowl and top it with shredded lettuce.
3. Combine the Parmesan cheese, mayo, and sugar in a bowl. Stir to combine. Spread on top.
4. Sprinkle with bacon and chill.
5. Toss lightly and serve.

BEETROOT SALAD

Preparation time: 15min
Cooking time: 15min

Servings: 4

Ingredients:

- 2 tbsp. Oil
- 1 lb. Beets, chopped (peeled)
- 1 Onion, chopped
- 2 tbsp. Lemon juice or Balsamic Vinegar
- Sugar to taste
- Black pepper to taste
- Salt to taste
- 1 tbsp. Parsley, minced
- ¼ cup of Water

Directions:

1. Turn on medium heat and place a skillet. Add oil and let it heat.

2. Once heated, add the onion and cook for 5 minutes.
3. Add the beats. Add water and vinegar. Cover the skillet and let it cook for 10 minutes.
4. Season with black pepper, salt, and sugar to taste. Lower the heat to low and stir just so that everything is combined.
5. Serve warm garnished with parsley. You can also serve it cold. Just make sure to refrigerate for a few hours.

VEGGIE SALAD

Preparation time: 20min
Cooking time: 30min

Servings: 6-10

Ingredients:

- 4 Potatoes, boiled and diced into tiny pieces
- Four carrots, cooked and diced into little pieces
- 5 Parsley roots, boiled and diced into tiny pieces
- Six eggs, hard-boiled, diced
- 1 Onion, chopped
- ½ jar Sour-tart pickles, chopped
- 7 tbsp. Dijon mustard
- 1 ½ cup Mayo
- Black pepper and salt to taste

Directions:

1. Boil the veggies and cut them into tiny pieces. Boil the eggs. Once cooled, dice them. Set aside.
2. Now, combine all ingredients and mix well in a bowl. Taste to see if you need to adjust seasoning. Refrigerate for upto 5 hours before serving or overnight if you want a creamier texture to add more mayo.
3. Serve and enjoy!

LEEK APPLE SALAD

Preparation time: 10min
Cooking time: 0 minutes

Servings: 2 -4

Ingredients:

- 1 tbsp. Parsley, minced
- 2 Apples, large
- 2 Leeks, just the white part
- 1 Lemon, the juice
- 1 tbsp. Oil (optional)
- One tbs. of Honey
- Black pepper and salt to taste

Directions:

1. Slice the leeks. Core and peel the apples. Slice them thinly.
2. Add the apples and leeks into a bowl. Add the remaining ingredients.
3. Stir and adjust seasoning if needed.
4. Let it sit for 1 hour so that the flavors can blend.
5. Serve!

TOMATO SALAD

Preparation time: 10min
Cooking time: 0 minutes

Servings: 6

Ingredients:

- 5 cups chopped tomatoes (heirloom)
- 4 cups green onions, chopped
- 4 tbsp. Fresh Basil, chopped
- ½ cup – 1 cup of Sour Cream
- ¼ tsp. Cayenne Pepper
- Black pepper and salt to taste

Directions:

1. Combine the chopped tomatoes and green onion in a bowl. Let it sit for 5 minutes. Don't pour off the juice.
2. Add the remaining ingredients and stir.
3. Taste and adjust seasoning if needed.
4. Serve as it is or spread on toasted bread. You can serve as a side dish too.

BUTTERED GREEN BEANS

Preparation time: 5min
Cooking time: 15min

Servings: 4

Ingredients:

- 20 oz. green beans
- 3 tsp. Butter
- ¼ cup Breadcrumbs
- Salt

Directions:

1. Cut the ends of the green beans and wash them. Boil for 10 minutes in salted water. Drain and keep them warm.
2. In a pan, place breadcrumbs. Cook until golden. Make sure to stir so that they don't burn. Once they become golden, add butter. Stir and melt.
3. Pour the butter mixture over the green beans.
4. Serve and enjoy!

POLISH ARTICHOKES

Preparation time: 10 min
Cooking time: 40min

Servings: 6-8

Ingredients:

- 3-4 Artichokes
- ½ lemon, the juice
- 1 tbsp. Oil
- 1 tsp. Sugar
- Two cloves of garlic
- 2 tsp. of thyme
- 1 tsp. of Oregano
- 1 cup red wine
- 2 tbsp. of Balsamic vinegar
- Black pepper and salt to taste

Directions:

1. Trim and cut off the top leaves and stems.
2. Add water to a pot and turn on medium-high heat. Once boiling, add the artichoke and add the remaining ingredients.
3. Cook for 40 minutes. Make sure to test it. It must be soft. Now drain well.
4. Serve as a side dish and with lemon and melted butter. Enjoy!

POLISH POPPY SEED COOKIES

Preparation time: 10 minutes

Cooking time: 50 minutes

Servings: 4

Ingredients:

- Two eggs
- 1 cup butter
- 3/4 cup white sugar
- 1 tsp. vanilla extract
- Two egg yolks
- 2 cups all-purpose flour
- 1/2 tsp. salt
- 1 tbsp. poppy seeds
- One egg white
- 1 tbsp. water

Directions:

1. In a medium saucepan, put the eggs and water to cover. Let it boil, then take off from heat and allow to cool. Take off the skin of the eggs, then remove the yolks. Break down the yolks and put them aside.
2. Beat the vanilla extract, sugar, and margarine or butter until it becomes creamy. Stir in the crumbled hard-boiled egg yolks and raw eggs yolks, then stir well. Slowly add salt and flour.
3. Let the dough chill in the fridge. Spread the dough into 1/4-inch thick using small amounts of dough. Slice the dough into 2-inch round shapes, then lay it on a greased cookie sheet.
4. Beat 1 tbsp. Of water and one egg white together. Use egg white glaze to brush the top surface of the cookies, then sprinkle poppy seeds on top.
5. Bake for 10-12 minutes at 175°C until it turns light brown.

POLISH STYLE LASAGNA

Preparation time: 10 minutes

Cooking time: 40 minutes

Servings: 4

Ingredients:

- Nine uncooked lasagna noodles
- One onion, sliced
- 1/2 cup butter
- 2 2/3 cups dry potato flakes
- 1 (8 oz.) package cream cheese

Directions:

1. Preheat oven to 175°Celcius (350°Farenheit).
2. Cook the noodles as specified on its package—drain water. Gently pat the noodles with a cloth to dry but keep them in a damp towel to keep a little moisture. Using a cooking spray or applying a little oil on each noodle can be an alternative to the wet towel.
3. Over medium heat, sauté onions for about 5 minutes in butter in a big skillet.
4. Prepare the instant mashed potatoes without using the milk as specified on the package. Blend the cream cheese into potatoes until combined well.
5. In a 13x9 inch baking pan greased lightly, lay three cooked noodles and pour half of the potato mixture on top. Repeat the layer ending with the last three noodles and the sautéed onions on top.
6. Place the dish in the heated oven (350°F or 175°C) and bake until the dish is bubbling, 20 minutes. Set aside for 5 minutes to cool before cutting. Serve.

APPLE, CABBAGE SMOKED SAUSAGE

Preparation time: 15min
Cooking time: 2h

Servings: 5

Ingredients:

- ¼ cup Brown Sugar, packed
- 1 Garlic clove, minced
- 1 tsp. Salt
- ¼ tsp. Nutmeg
- 1/8 tsp. Allspice
- 1/8 tsp. Black pepper
- ½ Cabbage head, chopped
- 12-16 oz. Chicken sausage or a different smoked sausage, sliced into pieces (1/2 inch)
- 1 cup Onion, sliced
- 1 Granny Smooth Apple, large, chopped (cored and peeled)
- ¼ cup of Apple juice
- 3 tbsp. Cider Vinegar

Directions:

1. Preheat the oven, 325F.
2. In a bowl, combine the black pepper, allspice, nutmeg, salt, garlic, and brown sugar.
3. In a Dutch oven (oven-safe) or casserole dish, add ½ cabbage, 1/2 sausages, ½ onion, and ½ apple. Sprinkle with ½ of the spice mixture and then repeat the process. Pour vinegar and apple juice.

4. Cover and let it bake for about 2 hours, stirring occasionally.
5. Serve!

POLISH HAMBURGERS

Preparation time: 20min
Cooking time: 30min

Servings: 4-6

Ingredients:

- One slice of White Bread, stale
- ¼ - ½ cup of Milk
- ¾ lb. of Ground beef
- ½ lb. ground pork
- 1 Onion, chopped (small)
- 1 Egg, beaten slightly
- Black pepper
- Salt

Directions:

1. In a bowl, place the bread slice and add milk. Let it soak until soft. Then add the egg, onion, pork, and beef. Season using black pepper and salt to taste. If it is too mushy, add 1-2 tbsp. Breadcrumbs.
2. Divide into 4-6 portions and form hamburger patties.
3. Add oil in a skillet and cook over medium-low until well done.
4. Make a hamburger sandwich or serve the patties with mushroom sauce and mashed potatoes.
5. Serve!

POLISH BREADED CUTLETS

Preparation time: 20min
Cooking time: 30min

Servings: 4

Ingredients:

- Four boneless Pork chops
- Black pepper and salt to taste
- 2 cups of Flour
- 1 Egg, (+1 tsp. Water and beaten)
- 2 cups of breadcrumbs
- 1 cup of Shortening

Directions:

1. Trim the gristle and the fat off the chops.
2. Pound the chops until a ¼ inch thick.
3. Coat the cutlets with flour, then egg and breadcrumbs. Let them sit for 10 minutes.
4. Heat the shortening in a skillet over medium heat. Fry the cutlets for 7 minutes on each side.
5. Serve warm with veggies, boiled potatoes, and applesauce. Enjoy!

WILD MUSHROOMS

Preparation time: 15min
Cooking time: 30min

Servings: 8

Ingredients:

- 7 cups of wild Mushrooms
- 2 Onion halved and then sliced
- 2 tbsp. Unsalted butter
- ½ cup of White wine
- ½ tsp. Thyme
- ½ tsp. marjoram
- ½ cup – 1 cup of sour cream
- 1 tbsp. Parsley, minced for garnish
- Black pepper and salt to taste
- 1 tbsp. flour

Directions:

1. Wash and dry the mushrooms. Slice thinly.
2. in a skillet over medium, melt the butter. Add the onions and cook for 10 minutes.
3. Add the mushrooms. Cook 5 minutes. Add wine, thyme marjoram, black pepper, and salt.
4. Add sour cream. Sprinkle the flour on top, so it doesn't crumble.
5. Simmer 15 minutes.
6. Serve garnished with parsley.
7. Enjoy!

EGGS STUFFED WITH KIELBASA

Preparation time: 10 minutes

Cooking time: 35 minutes

Servings: 4

Ingredients

- Eight hard-boiled eggs cooled and peeled
- ½ pound smoked kielbasa, skinned
- Two small onions, chopped
- ½ teaspoon paprika

- Two teaspoons chopped chives
- 6 Tablespoons mayonnaise
- Additional chopped chives for garnish

Directions

1. Remove the yolks from each egg by slicing it lengthwise.
2. Put the egg yolks into a food processor.
3. Cut the kielbasa into smaller pieces and add to the egg yolks.
4. Add the onions to the egg yolks and kielbasa.
5. Grind the egg yolks, kielbasa, and onion for 1 minute.
6. Transfer the mixture to a bowl.
7. Add the paprika to the mixture.
8. Add the chopped chives to the mixture.
9. Add the mayonnaise and mix until all ingredients are coated with mayonnaise. If the mixture seems too dry, add a little more mayonnaise.
10. Fill each egg with a generous amount of the kielbasa mixture.
11. Arrange the filled eggs on a serving platter.
12. Garnish with chopped chives.

Notes

- You can substitute sour cream for mayonnaise.

HONEY BREAD

Prep and Cook Time: 2 hours 30 minutes

Serving: 32

Serving: 32
Ingredients:

- 1 cup sugar
- 1 tsp. ground cinnamon
- 1/2 tsp. ground cloves
- 1/2 tsp. ground allspice
- Four eggs
- 1/2 cup milk
- 1/2 cup vegetable oil
- 1 tsp. baking soda
- 1 cup honey
- 4 cups all-purpose flour
- 1/2 cup raisins (optional)
- 1/2 cup chopped walnuts (optional)

Directions:

Mix the eggs, allspice, cloves, cinnamon, and sugar in a big bowl. Mix in the oil and milk, then stir in the baking soda. In a small pot, put the honey, then let it boil. Stir the honey, followed by the flour, into the bowl. Fold in the walnuts and raisins. Using a sturdy spoon, stir the mixture by hand for 10 minutes. Let the dough sit for an hour.

Set an oven to preheat at 165°C (325°F). Grease four 8x4-inch loaf pans lightly.

Fill each loaf pan with batter by about 2-inches. The bread will crack on top and be brown. Bake in the preheated oven for 1 hour and 15 minutes, until an inserted toothpick in the middle of the loaf exits clean.

POTATO DUMPLINGS

Preparation time: 10 minutes

Cooking time: 35 minutes

Servings: 4

Ingredients:

- 400g beets, cooked, peeled, cooled, and grated
- One teaspoon white vinegar
- One teaspoon brown sugar
- 2 cups horseradish
- 1/4 teaspoon salt

Directions:

1. Mix vinegar, brown sugar, horseradish, and salt until well combined in a large bowl. Mix in the beets completely.
2. Refrigerate for up to 2 weeks after packing into clean sterilised jars.
3. Serve warm or cold, although cold is more traditional.

CUCUMBER SALAD

Preparation time: 10 minutes

Cooking time: 0 minutes

Servings: 4

Ingredients:

- 400h small cucumbers, peeled and thinly sliced
- One bunch dill, chopped
- 2 1/2 tablespoons sour cream
- One teaspoon lemon juice
- One pinch of white sugar
- Salt and black pepper to taste

Directions:

In a dish, sprinkle salt over the cucumbers. Allow to stand for 5 minutes, or until cucumbers are tender. Cucumber liquid should be squeezed out and discarded. Cucumbers should be seasoned with dill.

In a mixing bowl, combine the sour cream, lemon juice, and sugar; add to the cucumbers and toss to coat—season with black pepper. Chill thoroughly before serving, at least 30 minutes.

MASHED POTATOES

Preparation time: 10 minutes

Cooking time: 40 minutes

Servings: 4

Ingredients:

- Six large potatoes
- 250ml milk (or sour cream)
- 25g butter
- Crushed cumin
- Salt
- Optionally: fried diced bacon

Directions:

1. Boil peeled diced potatoes for 30 minutes.
2. Meanwhile, heat the milk. Strain the water, add butter, and mash potatoes while pouring milk.

EGGS STUFFED WITH HERRING

Preparation time: 10 minutes

Cooking time: 30 minutes

Servings: 4

Ingredients

- Two salt herring fillets, skinned and soaked overnight **
- Eight hard-boiled eggs, peeled
- One teaspoon lemon juice

- 4 Tablespoons sour cream
- Two teaspoons onion, finely chopped
- Six teaspoon fresh chives, finely chopped
- One pickled cucumber, thinly sliced

Directions

1. Soak the fillets in a container of cold water overnight. Be sure to change the water every 6 to 8 hours.
2. Finely chop the herring and put it into a bowl.
3. Cut each hard-boiled eggs in half, lengthwise.
4. Carefully remove the egg yolks and set the egg whites aside.
5. Mash the egg yolks with a fork and add them to the bowl.
6. Add the lemon juice, sour cream, onion, and chives. Mix well.
7. Arrange the egg whites on a platter.
8. Fill the egg whites with the herring mixture.
9. Garnish with pickled cucumber slices.

Notes

- If you'd like a creamier mixture, you can add a little more sour cream

EGGS STUFFED WITH MUSHROOMS

Preparation time: 10 minutes

Cooking time: 40 minutes

Servings: 4

Ingredients

- 12 large, fresh mushrooms, washed and diced
- ½ onion, diced
- 2 Tablespoons unsalted butter
- Eight hard-boiled eggs cooled and peeled
- 4 Tablespoons mayonnaise
- Salt and pepper to taste
- Chopped fresh dill for garnish

Directions

1. Sauté the onions and mushrooms together in butter. Set aside to cool.
2. Slice each hard-boiled egg in half lengthwise.
3. Carefully remove the egg yolks and add them to a bowl.
4. Set the egg whites aside.
5. Mash the egg yolks with a fork.
6. Add the mushrooms, onion, and mayonnaise to the egg yolks. Mix well.
7. Salt and pepper the mixture to taste.
8. Place the egg whites on a platter.
9. Fill the egg whites with the mushroom mixture.

10. Garnish with fresh dill.

Notes

- You can substitute sour cream for the mayonnaise

GINGER SPICED CHRISTMAS COOKIES

Preparation time: 10 minutes

Cooking time: 30 minutes

Servings: 3

Ingredients

- 1 cup honey
- Four eggs
- ½ cup sugar
- 4 cups all-purpose white flour, sifted - OR - 4 cups all-purpose rye flour, sifted
- pinch of ground black pepper
- ½ teaspoon ground ginger
- ½ teaspoon ground cinnamon
- ½ teaspoon freshly ground nutmeg
- ½ teaspoon ground cloves
- ½ teaspoon ground allspice
- One teaspoon baking soda

Vanilla Glaze

- 1 Tablespoon water
- 7 ounces powdered sugar
- ¼ teaspoon vanilla extract

Vanilla Icing

- 2 cups powdered sugar
- Four tablespoons milk
- One teaspoon vanilla extract

Directions

1. Add the honey to a small saucepan and heat it. As soon as it starts to boil, remove the pan from the burner. Let the honey cool slightly.
2. Add the eggs and sugar to a bowl. Beat the eggs and sugar until the mixture starts to thicken.
3. Sift together the flour, pepper, ginger, cinnamon, nutmeg, cloves, allspice, and baking soda into the bowl of a stand mixer.
4. Gently add the egg and sugar mixture to the flour and spices and beat rapidly.
5. Add in the lukewarm honey and mix everything until the dough is smooth.
6. Wrap the dough in plastic wrap and refrigerate overnight.
7. When ready to make the cookies, preheat the oven to 350° F.
8. Turn the dough out onto a floured surface. Knead the dough for a minute.
9. Use a floured rolling pin to roll the dough out to 1/4-inch thickness.
10. Use cookie cutters to cut the dough into holiday shapes. Collect all of the scrap dough, roll it out again, and cut out more cookies.
11. If you'd like to hang some cookies as decorations, use a small knife to cut a round hole at the top of the cookie.
12. Prepare your cookie sheets with non-stick baking spray and parchment paper. Bake the cookies for about 12 minutes or until lightly browned.
13. Remove the cookies from the oven and allow them to cool completely before decorating.
14. For decorating, you can use the Vanilla Glaze to cover the top of each cookie. Or you can use the Vanilla Icing and a pastry bag to pipe decorations on each cookie.

Vanilla Glaze

1. In a bowl, slowly add the water to the sugar. Mix until you have a smooth paste. Add the vanilla extract and stir until it's incorporated.
2. Use a butter spreader or knife to apply the glaze to the cooled cookies.
3. Allow the glaze to dry.

Vanilla Icing

1. Put the powdered sugar into a large bowl.
2. Slowly add the milk to the sugar, stirring constantly.
3. Stir the vanilla extract into the sugar mixture. You want a thick but pourable consistency. If the icing is too thick, add a little bit more milk. If the icing is too thin, add a little more powdered sugar.
4. Transfer the icing to a pastry bag and decorate the cooled cookies.
5. Allow the icing to dry.

VANILLA PUDDING

Preparation time: 10 minutes

Cooking time: 20 minutes

Servings: 5

Ingredients

- One vanilla bean pod

- 4 cups milk, divided
- 6 Tablespoons vanilla sugar
- 2 Tablespoons butter
- Four egg yolks at room temperature
- 4 Tablespoons potato starch

Directions

1. Slice the vanilla bean pod lengthwise and scrape out the seeds.
2. Add 1-1/2 cup of milk, vanilla sugar, butter, and scraped vanilla seeds in a large pot.
3. Bring the milk mixture to a boil.
4. Add the remaining 2-1/2 cups of milk, egg yolks, and potato starch in a large bowl. Mix with a hand mixer until it's a smooth consistency.
5. Add the milk-egg yolk -potato starch mixture to the boiling milk in the pot. Reduce the heat and whisk the mixture to blend.
6. Cook and stir for another minute or until the mixture thicken.
7. Pour it into glass bowls.
8. You can eat this pudding either warm or cold.
9. You can also sprinkle the pudding with chocolate sprinkles, chocolate shavings, nuts, raisins, or anything you'd like.

POLISH SAUSAGE QUICHE

Preparation Time: 30 minutes
Cooking Time: 10 minutes
Serving: 4

Ingredients:

- Olive oil, two tablespoons
- Eggs, two
- Milk, half cup
- Quiche dough, as required
- Smoked sausage meat, one cup
- Chopped tomatoes, one cup
- Chopped cilantro, as required
- Mix spice powder, one teaspoon
- Onion, one cup
- Chopped garlic, one teaspoon
- Smoked paprika, half teaspoon
- Shredded cheddar cheese, one cup

Directions:

1. Take a frying pan.
2. Put the oil and onions.
3. Cook until the onions are tender and aromatic.
4. Add the tomatoes and garlic to it.
5. Add the spices.

6. When the tomatoes are done, add the sausage meat into it.
7. Mix the ingredients carefully and cover the pan.
8. Switch off the stove when the dish is cooked thoroughly.
9. When the mixture cools down, add the eggs and milk into it.
10. Lay the dough in a baking dish and pour the quiche mixture on top.
11. Add the shredded cheddar cheese on top.
12. Bake the quiche for twenty minutes.
13. Sprinkle the cilantro on top.
14. Your dish is ready to be served.

POLISH POTATO PANCAKES

Preparation Time: 10 minutes
Cooking Time: 15 minutes
Serving: 2

Ingredients:

- Fresh chopped cilantro, half cup
- Eggs, three
- Baking powder, one tablespoon
- Cooking oil, one tablespoon
- All-purpose flour, half cup
- Milk, half cup
- Black pepper, to taste
- Salt, as required
- Vanilla extract, one teaspoon
- Potatoes, half cup

Directions:

1. Add the eggs to a large bowl.
2. Mix the eggs until a smooth mixture is formed.
3. Add in the rest of the ingredients one by one, ensuring not to create any clusters.
4. Add in the potatoes, salt, and black pepper in the end.
5. Fold all the ingredients well.
6. Add the cooking oil to a pan.
7. Add some amount of the pancake mix into the pan and cook effectively.
8. Cook the pancakes on both sides until it turns golden brown.
9. The dish is ready to be served.

POLISH YEAST PANCAKES

Preparation Time: 10 minutes
Cooking Time: 15 minutes
Serving: 2

Ingredients:

- Eggs, three
- Cooking oil, one tablespoon
- All-purpose flour, half cup
- Milk, half cup
- Sugar, half cup
- Dry yeast, half teaspoon
- Salt, to taste
- Vanilla extract, one teaspoon

Directions:

1. Add the eggs to a large bowl.
2. Mix the eggs until a smooth mixture is formed.
3. Add in the rest of the ingredients one by one, ensuring not to create any clusters.
4. Fold all the ingredients well.
5. Add the cooking oil to a pan.
6. Add some amount of the pancake mix into the pan and cook effectively.
7. Cook the pancakes on both sides until it turns golden brown.
8. The dish is ready to be served.

EGG SCRAMBLE WITH SAUSAGE

Preparation time: 12 minutes

Cooking time: 30 minutes

Servings: 4

Ingredients

- 6 ounces smoked sausage, sliced 1/4-inch thick
- 1/2 medium onion, chopped
- Two medium potatoes, peeled, cut into 1/2-inch cubes
- Two tablespoons unsalted butter
- 1/2 medium green pepper, seeded, chopped
- 1 1/2 cups of sliced mushrooms
- Six large eggs
- Salt and pepper
- 1/4 cup of whole milk

Directions:

Place the potatoes and two teaspoons salt in a large, deep skillet and cover with 1-inch cold water. Bring to a boil and cook for 7-9 minutes or until potatoes are just tender. Drain and wipe the skillet clean.

Melt butter in the same skillet over medium-high heat. Add the sausage. Cook, occasionally stirring for 3-4 minutes or until browned on both sides. Remove from the skillet with a slotted spoon and place in a bowl. Add the vegetables to the pan; season with salt and pepper. Cook over medium heat, occasionally stirring, for 7-9 minutes or until the mushrooms are browned, and the vegetables are tender.

Beat the eggs with milk in a bowl—season with salt and pepper. Add sausage and potatoes to vegetables in a skillet and stir to combine. Pour in the egg mixture and cook, constantly stirring for 1-3 minutes or until the eggs are set but still creamy. Serve immediately.

APPLE PANCAKES

Preparation time: 10min
Cooking time: 25min

Servings: 6

Ingredients:

- 5 Apples
- 1 cup Flour
- ½ tsp. of Salt
- 1 cup of Milk
- 1 Egg
- 1 tsp. Oil
- 1 tbsp. Sugar
- Sweet Syrup or Powdered Sugar
- ½ tsp. baking powder

Directions:

1. combine the sugar, flour, salt, and baking soda in a large bowl.
2. In a medium-size, bowl beat the egg lightly and add the oil and milk. Mix well. Add to the dry ingredients. Stir until you get a smooth batter.
3. Slice the apples into circles. Place a pan over medium heat and add ½ tsp Butter.
4. Deep each apple slice into the pancake batter and place it on the pan to cook. Once it starts to form, bubbles turn. Cook for 1-2 more minutes and set aside.
5. Drizzle with sweet syrup or sprinkle with powdered sugar and serve.

POLISH PANCAKES WITH PORK AND MUSHROOMS

Preparation Time: 10 minutes
Cooking Time: 15 minutes
Serving: 2

Ingredients:

- Fresh chopped cilantro, half cup
- Eggs, three
- Chopped mushrooms, half cup
- Baking powder, one tablespoon
- Cooking oil, one tablespoon
- All-purpose flour, half cup
- Milk, half cup
- Black pepper, to taste
- Salt, as required
- Ground pork meat, half cup

Directions:

1. Add the eggs to a large bowl.
2. Mix the eggs until a smooth mixture is formed.
3. Add in the rest of the ingredients one by one, ensuring not to start any clusters.
4. Add in the pork meat, mushrooms, salt, and black pepper in the end.
5. Fold all the ingredients well.
6. Add the cooking oil to a pan.
7. Add some amount of the pancake mix into the pan and cook effectively.
8. Cook the pancakes on both sides until it turns golden brown.
9. The dish is ready to be served.

POLISH BRAIDED EASTER EGG BREAD

Preparation Time: 30 minutes
Cooking Time: 30 minutes
Serving: 10

Ingredients:

- Whole milk, a quarter cup
- Refined sugar, one and a half cup
- Bread flour, five-pound
- Salt, to taste
- Unsalted butter, one cup
- Eggs, ten
- Water, two cups
- Egg wash, one
- Active yeast, two packets

Directions:

1. Add all the ingredients into a bowl.
2. Mix all the ingredients well.
3. Make a dough structure from the mixture.
4. Roll out the dough into a log.
5. Cut the log into three strands that are joined at a corner.
6. Braid the dough and place it on a greased baking tray.
7. Bake the bread for thirty minutes or until it achieves a golden-brown color.
8. Slice the bread.
9. Your dish is ready to be served.

POLISH PACZKI DONUTS

Preparation Time: 10 minutes
Cooking Time: 30 minutes
Serving: 6

Ingredients:

- Eggs, eight
- Butter, half cup
- Sugar, two cups
- Flour, three cups
- Milk, one cup
- Baking powder, one tablespoon
- Sour cream, two tablespoons
- Baking soda, one teaspoon

For icing:

- Mixed berry jam, one cup
- Icing sugar, one cup

Directions:

1. Stir all the ingredients well in a large basin.
2. Form semi-thick dough from the mixture.
3. Heat a pan full of oil.
4. Make a round doughnut-like structure with the help of a doughnut cutter.
5. Fry the doughnuts.
6. Cool down the doughnuts.
7. Add the icing sugar all over the doughnuts.
8. Add the berry jam in between the doughnuts through a piping bag.
9. Your dish is ready to be served.

CHOCOLATE HOMEMADE POLISH PUDDING

Preparation time: 10min
Cooking time: 10min

Servings: 1

Ingredients:

- 1 cup Milk
- 1 tsp. unsalted Butter
- 2 tbsp. Sugar
- 1 ½ tbsp. Potato Starch
- 1 tbsp. Flour
- One egg yolk
- 2 tbsp. Cocoa powder, unsweetened

Directions:

1. In a pot, pour just ¾ cup of milk. Add the sugar and butter. Turn on medium-high heat. They were once boiling turn off the heat.
2. The remaining milk mixes with cocoa powder, potato starch, flour, and yolk. Mix until smooth.
3. Add the batter into the pot. Stir while pouring.
4. Warm it before serving.
5. Serve cold or warm and enjoy!

APPLE CAKE

Preparation time: 30min
Cooking time: 50min

Servings: 20

Ingredients: For the top and the bottom layers:

- Two butter sticks, soft
- 3 cups flour
- Two eggs
- 2 tsp. baking powder
- 1 tsp. Vanilla extract
- ¾ cup Sugar
- 2 tbsp. Sour Cream

Batter mix:

- 2 lb. Apples, blended (the juice squeezed out)
- 2 tbsp. Potato starch
- 1 cup of Apple sauce
- 1 tsp. Cinnamon

Glaze:

- 1 ½ cups Sugar
- 2-4 tbsp. Milk
- 2 tsp. Vanilla extract

Directions:

1. Combine the ingredients for the batter in a large bowl. They mix well until smooth. Divide in half—place ½ batter in a baking pan and the other ½ in the refrigerator.
2. Core and chop the apples. If you want, you can peel them. Blend them but leave chunks too. Drain well. Add cinnamon, applesauce, and potato starch. Mix well.
3. Turn on the oven to 365F. Bake 1.2 of the batter for 20min. Now take it out, add the apple filling top with the remaining batter from the fridge. Bake 30 minutes.
4. In a bowl, combine the ingredients for the glaze. Mix well. Spread on the cake.
5. Cut and serve!

CARAMELIZED ONION PIEROGIES

Preparation time: 10 minutes

Cooking time: 55 minutes

Servings: 4

Ingredients for the dough:

- 2 cups of whole milk
- One egg, large
- One stick of butter
- 1 tsp. of salt
- 3 cups + 2 cups of all-purpose flour

Ingredients for the filling:

- 6-7 potatoes, peeled and cut into quarters
- One onion, chopped
- Dash of salt
- Dash of black pepper
- ½ tsp. of powdered garlic
- 2 Tbsp. of the oil from the onions

Ingredients for topping:

- Sour cream, for topping
- Green onions, sliced and for topping

Directions:

1. In the large bowl of a stand mixer, add the whole milk, a large egg, a dash of salt, and three cups of milk. Beat on the lowest setting until mixed.
2. Add in two cups of flour and stir well to mix.
3. Add in the butter and knead the dough with your hands until smooth. Cover the dough and set it aside to rise for 30 minutes.
4. Place a large skillet over medium heat. Add in the oil, and once hot, add in the onions. Cook for 10 to 15 minutes or until caramelized. Remove from heat and set aside.

5. Add a large pot over medium heat. Fill with water and bring to a boil. Once it comes to a boil, gently add the potatoes—Cook for 15 to 20 minutes or until soft. Drain and transfer to a bowl. Mash until smooth in consistency.

6. Add half of the caramelized onions into the bowl with the mashed potatoes. Add in the powdered garlic and black pepper. Stir well to mix. Add in a touch of oil and stir again. Set aside.

7. Roll out the dough on a lightly floured surface until 1/8 inch thick. Cut out 3 to 4-inch circles from the dough.

8. Add a teaspoon of the mashed potato filling into the center. To seal the dough, turn it over and crimp the edges with a fork. Repeat.

9. Place a large pot over medium heat. Fill with salted water and bring to a boil. Once boiling, add in the pierogies. Cook for 2 to 3 minutes or until the pierogies float to the surface. Remove and place onto a large plate lined with paper towels to drain.

10. Serve the pierogies with a topping of the remaining caramelized onions. Serve with some sour cream and sliced green onions.

MUSHROOM AND SPINACH PIEROGIES

Preparation time: 10 minutes

Cooking time: 50 minutes

Servings: 4

Ingredients for the dough:

- Two eggs
- ¼ cup of sour cream
- 1 cup of water
- 1 tsp. of sea salt
- 3 ½ cups of all-purpose flour, evenly divided

Ingredients for the filling:

- 1 Tbsp. of extra virgin olive oil
- ½ of a yellow onion, chopped
- Two cloves of garlic, minced
- 3 cups of cremini mushrooms, chopped
- 1 cup of spinach leaves
- 2 tbsp. of parsley, chopped
- 1 tsp. of sea salt
- 1 Tbsp. of canola oil

Ingredients for the topping:

- ¼ cup of sour cream
- Two green onions, chopped

Directions:

1. Add in the eggs, sour cream, water, and a dash of sea salt in a medium bowl. Stir well to mix. Add in the three ¼ cups of all-purpose flour and stir well until incorporated.

2. Place a medium skillet over medium heat. Add in the minced garlic and cook for another 2 minutes.
3. Add in the mushrooms and toss well to mix—Cook for 10 minutes. Add in the spinach and fold gently to incorporate—Cook for 1 to 2 minutes or until wilted. Add in the chopped parsley and season with a dash of sea salt.
4. Place the dough back onto a lightly floured surface and roll out until ¼ inch in thickness. Cut out 3 to 4-inch circles.
5. Place 1 to 2 teaspoons of the filling into the center of each circle. Moisten the edges of the rings and fold over the filling. To seal the edges, crimp them with a fork. Repeat with the remaining dumplings.
6. Place the dumplings onto a large baking sheet.
7. Place a large saucepan over medium heat. Add in the canola oil, and once hot, add in the dumplings—Cook for 2 to 3 minutes on each side or until browned. Remove and transfer to a large plate lined with paper towels to drain.
8. Serve with a topping of sour cream and chopped green onions.

POTATO AND SAUERKRAUT PIEROGI

Preparation time: 10 minutes

Cooking time: 40 minutes

Servings: 4

Ingredients for the Filling:

- 1 pound of russet potatoes, thinly sliced
- Dash of salt
- Dash of black pepper
- 1, 14.4 ounce can of sauerkraut
- 2 Tbsp. of extra virgin olive oil

Ingredients for the dough:

- 2 ½ cups of bread flour
- 1 tsp. of baking powder
- Dash of salt
- 1 cup of sour cream
- One egg, large
- One egg yolk

Ingredients for the topping:

- 4 Tbsp. of extra virgin olive oil
- One onion, sliced
- ½ tsp. of salt

Directions:

1. In a large pot, add in the sliced potatoes. Cover with 6 cups of water and set over high heat. Bring to a boil and reduce the heat to medium—Cook for 15 minutes or until soft. Drain and add into a large bowl of a stand mixer.
2. In the same bowl, add in the sauerkraut and two tablespoons of olive oil—season with a dash of salt and black pepper.
3. Beat on the medium setting until thoroughly mashed. Set mixture aside for later use.

4. In another large bowl of a stand mixer, add bread flour, baking powder, and a dash of salt. Stir well until mixed. Add in the sour cream, egg, and egg yolk. Stir until evenly mixed.
5. Transfer the dough onto a lightly floured surface. Knead for 1 minute or until smooth.
6. Spread the dough until 1/8 inch in thickness and cut out 3-inch circles from the dough. Add a teaspoon of the filling onto each ring. To seal, wrap the dough over the filling and crimp the edges with a fork. Repeat with the remaining dough and filling.
7. Place a large skillet over medium heat. Add four tablespoons of olive oil into the skillet. Once hot, add in the onion. Season with a dash of salt and cook for 15 minutes or until the onions are browned. Remove from heat.
8. Place a large pot over medium heat. Fill with 4 quarts of water and a dash of salt. Bring the water to a boil. Add in the pierogies and cook for 5 minutes or until they begin to float to the surface. Remove and drain.
9. Add the pierogies into the skillet with the onions and place over medium heat. Cook for 5 minutes or until the pierogies are browned on both sides.
10. Remove from heat and serve immediately.

VEGAN PIEROGI

Preparation time: 10 minutes

Cooking time: 60 minutes

Servings: 4

- Ingredients for the dough:
- 1 ½ cups of all-purpose flour
- ½ cup of water, boiled

Ingredients for the filling:

- 2 to 3 Tbsp. of vegetable oil
- Two onions, chopped
- 14 ounces of potatoes
- 9 ounces of mushrooms
- Four cloves of garlic, minced
- 1 tsp. of salt
- Dash of black pepper
- Two green onions, thinly sliced and for serving
- Sauerkraut, for serving

Ingredients for the cashew cream:

- 1 cup of raw cashews, soaked
- ¾ cup of water
- 3 Tbsp. of lemon juice
- 2 tsp. of apple cider vinegar
- 2 tsp. of soy sauce
- 2 tsp. of salt

Directions:

1. Add in the all-purpose flour in a large bowl and pour the water over the top. Stir well to mix.
2. Transfer the dough onto a flat surface dusted with flour, and knead for 1 to 2 minutes or until the dough is smooth in consistency. Cover and set aside to rest for 30 minutes.

3. Place a large pan over medium to high heat. Add in a spoonful of the vegetable oil. Once hot, add in the onions. Cook for 5 minutes or until transparent.
4. Place a large pot over medium heat and fill with water. Bring to a boil. Add in the potatoes and boil for 15 to 20 minutes. Drain the potatoes and add them to a bowl. Mash until smooth in consistency.
5. Place a large grill pan over high heat. Once hot, add the mushrooms and grill for 10 minutes or until soft. Remove and transfer to a large plate to cool.
6. Add the garlic, onions, and mushrooms to the potatoes. Season with a dash of salt and black pepper. Stir well to mix.
7. Spread out the dough until it is 1/8 inch thick on a lightly floured board. Cut out 4-inch circles from the dough. Add a teaspoon of the filling onto each dough. To seal, wrap the dough over the filling and crimp the edges with a fork. Repeat.
8. Place a large pot over medium to high heat. Fill with water and bring to a boil. Add in the pierogies and cook for 5 minutes or until they begin to float to the surface. Remove from the oven and place on a platter lined with paper towels to drain.
9. Place a large skillet over medium heat. Add in a touch of oil, and once hot, add in the pierogies—Cook for 5 minutes on each side or until browned.
10. Serve immediately with the cream poured over the top. Serve with the sauerkraut and green onions.

PAD THAI PIEROGIES

Preparation time: 10 minutes

Cooking time: 30 minutes

Servings: 4

Ingredients:

- 1, a 12-ounce box of potato and cheddar miniature pierogies
- 1 Tbsp. of butter
- Two eggs, large and beaten
- 1 Tbsp. of peanut oil
- One clove of garlic, minced
- 1 pound chicken breasts, boneless, skinless, and cut into thin slices
- ½ tsp. of salt
- ¼ tsp. of crushed red pepper flakes
- ½ cup of peanut sauce
- 1 cup of bean sprouts
- ¼ cup of peanuts, chopped
- Two scallions, sliced thinly

Directions:

1. Boil the pierogies according to the directions on the package.
2. Place a large skillet over medium to high heat. Add in the butter, and once melted, add in the eggs—Cook for 1 to 2 minutes or until scrambled. Transfer into a medium bowl.
3. In the same skillet, add in the peanut oil. Once hot, immediately add the garlic and cook for 1 to 2 minutes or until browned. Transfer the garlic into the bowl with the scrambled eggs.
4. In the same skillet, add the chicken slices—season with a dash of salt and crushed red pepper flakes.
5. Add the egg mixture, fresh peanut sauce, bean sprouts, and pierogies. Toss well to mix.
6. Remove from heat and serve with a garnish of chopped peanuts and sliced scallions.

VEGAN SWEET POTATO PIEROGIES

Preparation time: 10 minutes

Cooking time: 50 minutes

Servings: 4

Ingredients for the dough:

- 3 cups of all-purpose flour
- 1 tsp. of sea salt
- 1 cup of water
- 1 Tbsp. of vegetable oil
- ¼ to ½ cup of all-purpose flour

Ingredients for the filling:

- 3 ½ cup of sweet potato, peeled and cut into small cubes
- Two cloves of garlic, minced
- 2 Tbsp. of nutritional yeast
- 2 Tbsp. of vegan butter
- ½ tsp. of dill
- ¼ tsp. of dried sage
- ¼ tsp. of sea salt
- ¼ tsp. of black pepper
- 1/3 cup of sauerkraut

Directions:

1. Place a large pot over medium to high heat. Fill with water and season with a dash of salt. Bring to a boil and add in the sweet potato. Cook for 10 minutes or until the sweet potatoes are soft.
2. In a large bowl, add in the all-purpose flour and sea salt. Stir well to mix and add in the water and oil. Stir well to combine.
3. Divide the dough in half and wrap each half individually in plastic wrap. Place into the fridge to chill.
4. Drain the sweet potatoes and place them into a large bowl. Mash until smooth in consistency. Add in the remaining filling ingredients except for the sauerkraut. Stir well to mix. Place into the fridge to chill.
5. Stretch out every piece of dough until it is 1/8 inch thick. Cut out 3 to 4-inch circles from the dough.
6. In each circle, add ½ to ¾ tablespoon of the sweet potato filling. Fold the dough over the filling. Crimp the edges with a fork to seal. Transfer onto a plate baking sheet lined with a sheet of parchment paper.
7. Place a large pot over medium to high heat. Raise salted water to a boil in a large pot. Add in the pierogies and boil for 2 to 3 minutes or until they begin to float to the surface. Remove and place onto a large plate lined with paper towels.
8. Place a large skillet over medium heat. Add in the vegan butter, and once melted, add in the pierogies—Cook for 2 to 3 minutes or until golden browned.
9. Remove from heat. Serve with sour cream and sauerkraut.

POTATO PIEROGIES WITH HORSERADISH CREAM

Preparation time: 10 minutes

Cooking time: 45 minutes

Servings: 4

Ingredients for the pierogies:

- Five russet potatoes, unpeeled and sliced thinly
- 4 cups of all-purpose flour, extra for rolling
- ¼ cup of sour cream
- 1 tsp. of salt, evenly divided
- 1 cup of water
- ¼ tsp. of black pepper
- 3 Tbsp. of canola oil
- ¾ of a yellow onion, chopped
- 3 Tbsp. of extra virgin olive oil
- 3 Tbsp. coconut milk
- ½ cup of extra virgin olive oil, evenly divided and for frying

Ingredients for the cream:

- 2 Tbsp. of extra virgin olive oil
- ¼ of a yellow onion, chopped
- ¼ cup of horseradish jarred and hot
- Six capers, drained
- 1 Tbsp. of Dijon mustard
- 2 Tbsp. of agave nectar
- 1 Tbsp. of rice wine vinegar
- 6 ounces of silk tofu, firm

Directions:

1. Place a large pot over medium to high heat. Fill with salted water and bring the water to a boil. Add in the potatoes and boil for 10 to 15 minutes or soft. Drain and set aside.
2. Add in the all-purpose flour, a dash of salt, and black pepper in a large bowl. Stir well to mix.
3. Add in the sour cream and stir well until incorporated.
4. Knead the dough for 5 minutes or until smooth. Form the dough into a ball and place it into a ball. Cover and set aside to rest for 20 to 30 minutes.
5. Place a small saucepan over medium heat. Add in the olive oil, and once hot, add in the onion and cook for 5 minutes or until soft. Add the horseradish, capers, Dijon mustard, agave nectar, and rice wine vinegar. Stir well to mix and continue to cook for 2 minutes.
6. Transfer to a bowl and place into the fridge to cool.
7. Place a large skillet over medium heat. Add in the canola oil, and once hot, add in the onion. Remove and add coconut milk, extra virgin olive oil, and a dash of salt. Stir well to mix before adding in the potatoes. Mash until smooth in consistency. Set aside.
8. Spread out the dough until it is 1/8 inch thick on a lightly floured board. Cut out 3 to 4-inch circles from the dough. Add a teaspoon of the filling into the center of each circle. Fold the dough over the filling and crimp the edges to seal. Repeat with the remaining potato filling and dough.
9. Place a separate large skillet over medium heat. Add ¼ cup of olive oil to it. Once hot, add in the pierogies—Cook for 4 minutes on each side or until browned. Remove and place onto a plate lined with paper towels to drain.
10. Serve the pierogies with chilled horseradish cream.

COTTAGE CHEESE PIEROGIES

Preparation time: 10 minutes

Cooking time: 40 minutes

Servings: 4

Ingredients for the filling:

- 9 ounces of potatoes, cut into thin slices
- 3 Tbsp. of extra virgin olive oil
- One onion, chopped
- 9 ounces of cottage cheese

Ingredients for the dough:

- 9 ounces of self-rising flour, extra for dusting
- 1 tsp. of salt
- 1 Tbsp. of vegetable oil
- 5 ounces of warm water

Ingredients for serving:

- Sour cream, for topping
- Dill, chopped, and for garnish

Directions:

1. Place a large pot over medium to high heat. Fill with salted water and allow to come to a boil. Gently add the potatoes and cook for 15 to 20 minutes or until soft. Drain and transfer to a large bowl.
2. Add in the flour, salt, vegetable oil, and water in a large bowl. Stir well to mix.
3. Place the dough onto a lightly floured surface and knead for 1 to 2 minutes or until smooth in consistency.
4. Place a large skillet over medium heat. Add in the oil, and once hot, add in the chopped onions. Cook for 5 minutes or until soft. Transfer into a large bowl with the potatoes.
5. In the same bowl, add in the cottage cheese. Mash until smooth in consistency.
6. Spread out the dough until it is 1/8 inch thick on a lightly floured board. Cut out 3 to 4-inch circles from the dough.
7. Add a teaspoon of the cottage cheese filling into the circles of dough. Fold the dough over and crimp the edges with a fork. Repeat with the remaining filling and dough circles.
8. Place a large pot over medium heat. Raise salted water to a boil in a large pot. Add in the pierogies and cook for 2 to 3 minutes or until the pierogies begin to float to the surface. Remove and place onto a large plate lined with paper towels to drain.
9. Serve immediately with a topping of sour cream and chopped dill.

MAZUREK FINGERS

Preparation time: 10 minutes

Cooking time: 40 minutes

Servings: 4

Ingredients for Fingers

- Three eggs, separated

- 1/2 cup fine sugar
- 1/2 cup all-purpose flour
- 1/2-pound semi-sweet chocolate, coarsely grated
- 1 cup ground almonds

Ingredients for Decoration

- 1 1/3 cup red currant jelly
- 2/3 cup semi-sweet chocolate, broken into pieces
- 1/4 cup unsalted butter

Directions

1. Preheat the oven to 400 degrees (F).
2. Line and grease an 11" x 7" pan.
3. Cream the egg yolks and sugar in a large bowl until pale yellow and thick. Slowly fold in the flour a little at a time.
4. Whisk the egg whites until stiff and fold them into the flour mixture in a small bowl.
5. Gently add the chocolate and almonds to the flour mixture.
6. Place the mixture into the tin and spread it out evenly.
7. Bake for 20-25 minutes at 400 degrees (F). until lightly browned.
8. Cool in the tin for 5 minutes and then turn out onto a wire rack to cool.
9. Warm the jelly in a bowl over hot water and spread over the Mazurek to decorate.
10. Let it set completely, and then chill for about 20 minutes.
11. In another bowl, over hot water, melt the chocolate and butter. Remove from the heat and let cool for just a few minutes so that the mixture does not thicken.
12. Pour the chocolate on top of the Mazurek and spread it evenly.
13. Let it set completely before cutting the pastry into fingers.

GREAT-AUNT DAISY'S DATE ROLLS

Preparation time: 10 minutes

Cooking time: 30 minutes

Servings: 4

Ingredients

- 1 cup of butter
- 1/2 lb. of cream cheese
- 2 cups of sifted flour
- 1/4 teaspoon of salt
- confectioners' sugar
- pitted dates

Directions

1. Preheat oven to 375 degrees (F).
2. In a large bowl, cream the butter and cream cheese together. Slowly blend in the flour and salt.
3. Place the dough in the refrigerator and chill for several hours.
4. Sprinkle surface with powdered sugar. Spread dough to 1/4-inch thickness, and with a sharp knife or pastry, wheel cut into strips that are 1-inch wide and 3-inches long.
5. Place a date in the center of each strip and roll the dough up.

6. Place the date roll-up folded side down on a cookie sheet.
7. Bake at 375 degrees (F). for 12-15 minutes or until the roll-up is light brown. Take from the oven and allow to cool.
8. Once the pastries have cooled, sprinkle with powdered sugar. Makes 30-40 pastries.

CHRISTMAS EVE LAMANCE

Preparation time: 10 minutes

Cooking time: 20 minutes

Servings: 4

Ingredients for Pastry

- 1 1/2 cups all-purpose flour
- Two tablespoons butter
- pinch of confectioners' sugar
- One egg yolk
- Three tablespoons sour cream

Ingredients for Dip

- 2/3 cup poppy seeds, ground twice
- 1/4 cup ground almonds
- Two tablespoons honey
- One ¼ cups sour cream

Directions for Pastry

1. Lightly grease baking sheets.
2. In a large bowl, sift the flour and cut in the butter. Stir in the sugar, egg yolk, and sour cream. Mix until a soft dough forms.
3. Divide the dough in half and carefully cover each piece in plastic wrap. Place in the refrigerator for about 15 minutes.
4. Preheat oven to 350 degrees (F).
5. Roll out the dough about 1/4-inch thin. Cut into squares and then in half to make triangles. Continue until all of the dough has been used.
6. Place the pastry on the baking sheets and bake for about 8-10 minutes or until golden brown. Remove from oven and cool pie on wire racks.

Directions for Dip

1. Mix all ingredients, and then add 4 or 5 crushed pastries into the mixture. Mix well. Place dip in a small bowl and place pastries on a plate around the bowl for dipping.

POLISH NUT TARTS

Preparation time: 10 minutes

Cooking time: 30 minutes

Servings: 4

Ingredients for Tart Shell

- 3/4 cup butter
- 2 3/4 cups all-purpose flour

- 2/3 cup confectioners' sugar
- Four egg yolk
- One teaspoon vanilla

Ingredients for Filling

- Three eggs, separate
- handful of walnuts
- 1/2 cup jam (your choice)

Directions for Tart Shells

2. Preheat oven to 400 degrees (F).
3. Combine the butter, flour, confectioners' sugar, egg yolks, and vanilla in a large bowl. Mix well.
4. On a floured surface, roll out the dough about 1/4 inch thick.
5. Cut out circles to fit into individual tart pans with a cookie cutter or a floured upside-down glass.
6. Place tart pans with the dough into the oven and bake for 8-10 minutes or until golden. Remove from oven and cool.
7. Reduce the temperature range of the oven to 325 degrees (F).

Directions for Filling

1. Beat egg yolks, sugar, and vanilla for about 5 minutes in a small bowl.
2. In another small bowl, beat the egg whites until they become stiff. Fold in the walnuts and mix gently.
3. Spread about 1/2 teaspoon of jam on the bottom of each tart and then top with the filling mixture.
4. Place tarts back into the oven and bake for another 10-12 minutes at 325 degrees (F).
5. Makes two dozen tarts.

AUNT SABINA'S POLISH STYLE APPLE PIE

Preparation time: 10 minutes

Cooking time: 30 minutes

Servings: 4

Ingredients for the Filling

- 8-10 baking apples, peeled and cored, cut into cubes
- One tablespoon lemon juice
- Two tablespoons sugar
- One teaspoon vanilla

Ingredients for the Pastry

- 1 1/2 cups all-purpose flour
- 3/4 cup butter, chopped
- 1/2 cup light brown sugar
- 1/2 teaspoon salt
- Three egg yolks
- Two tablespoons sour cream

Directions for Filling

1. In a bowl, toss the chopped apples with the lemon juice.

2. In a large skillet, cook the apples for about 10 minutes until the apples are soft over medium-high heat. Remove from heat and set aside.

Directions for the Pastry

1. Preheat oven to 350 degrees (F).
2. Lightly butter an 8" round cake pan.
3. In a large bowl, combine the flour and butter. Mix until it has the consistency of bread crumbs. Mix in the sugar and salt. Add the egg yolks and sour cream. Mix until dough-like. Refrigerate for about an hour.
4. Using about 2/3 of the pastry dough, roll it out into a circle. Using this dough, cover the bottom and sides of the pan. Fork the pastry shell and prebake it for 12 minutes in 350 degrees (F) oven. Remove from oven and let cool.
5. Roll the remaining pastry about 1/4-inch thick and cut it into strips about 1/2 wide using a knife or pastry wheel.
6. Spread the apples evenly through the pastry shell. Place the pastry strips on top of the apples parallel to each other so that there is little space between each strip.
7. Bake the pie for about 25-30 min, till the top is golden brown. Remove from the oven and let cool. Then it easily cuts into pretty lovely pieces.
8. This dessert is delicious as is or served with vanilla ice cream.

COFFEE CAKE

Preparation time: 10 minutes

Cooking time: 30 minutes

Servings: 4

Ingredients

- Cake
- ½ cup unsalted butter
- ½ cup sugar
- Two packages of active dry yeast
- 1-1/2 cups milk
- One teaspoon salt
- Five large eggs at room temperature
- ½ teaspoon vanilla
- Zest of one lemon
- 6 cups all-purpose flour
- 1 cup raisins (optional)
- Crumb Topping
- 1 cup granulated sugar
- 1 cup all-purpose flour
- ½ cup cold butter

Directions

1. Add the sugar and butter to a large bowl.
2. Put the milk in a heavy saucepan and turn the heat to medium. As it heats, stir the milk with a wooden or heatproof spatula. Use a candy thermometer to note when the milk reaches 180° F. When it does, continue to heat

it for 15 seconds. Other signs that the milk is at 180° F include tiny bubbles around the edge of the pan, a little steam, and thin foam on the surface of the milk.

3. Remove the pan from the heat. Pour the milk into the bowl with the butter and sugar. Stir with a wooden spoon until the butter melts. Allow this mixture to cool to 105° F.
4. Add the yeast to the warm milk mixture and mix well.
5. Using a small bowl, whisk the eggs and salt together. Add the vanilla and lemon zest to the eggs and stir. Set aside.
6. Mix half of the flour into the milk mixture. Add the raisins if you're using them.
7. Add the egg mixture to the flour and milk. Continue to add in the remaining flour. Keep folding the dough until everything is blended.
8. Grease a large baking pan. Turn the dough into the pan. Make sure it's evenly distributed throughout the pan. Cover with a clean towel and set aside in a warm (not hot) area. Allow the dough to double in size, taking 1 to 2 hours.
9. Preheat the oven to 300° F
10. Make the Topping
11. Mix the flour and sugar in a medium bowl. Cut the butter into the flour and sugar until you get a crumbly mixture.
12. Spread the topping on the top of the cake.
13. Bake the Cake
14. Bake the cake in the oven for 50 minutes. when cake tester or toothpick comes out clean, remove the cake from the oven.
15. Allow the cake to cool in the pan for 10 minutes. Then move the cake on a cooling rack until completely cooled.
16. Slice and serve.

POLISH POVITICA HOLIDAY BREAD

Preparation time: 10 minutes

Cooking time: 50 minutes

Servings: 6

Ingredients for the Sweet Dough:

- 1 ½ cups of lukewarm milk
- ½ cup of white sugar
- 2 tsp. salt
- Two large eggs
- ¼ cup of soft butter
- Two packs of active dry yeast
- ½ cup of water
- 7 ½ to 8 cups of all-purpose flour

Ingredients for the Filling:

- 1 4 ounces can of evaporated milk
- 1 ½ cups of white sugar
- 1 cup of margarine
- 1 ½ pound of ground pecans
- Four large eggs
- Pinch of salt

- 1 tsp. cocoa
- 1 tsp. ground cinnamon

Directions:

1. First, prepare the sweet dough. For this, use a large bowl and add in the lukewarm milk, white sugar, salt, soft butter, and large eggs. Whisk until evenly mixed.
2. Then, add the water and yeast into a small bowl. Stir to dissolve and allow it to rest for 5 minutes or until foamy.
3. Use a large bowl and add half of the all-purpose flour. Pour in the yeast mixture and milk mixture. Stir until dough begins to form. Transfer the dough on a lightly floured surface. Knead until soft. Place the dough in a large greased bowl and cover. Allow it to rise for 1 hour or when the dough has doubled in size.
4. After this time, punch down your dough and allow it to rise again for another hour or when the dough has doubled in size.
5. Divide the dough into three equal-sized pieces. Roll each piece into a large rectangle.
6. Make the filling next. To do this, use a medium bowl and add in all ingredients for the filling. Stir to evenly mix and spread in the center of each dough rectangle. Make a huge log out of the dough and twist in a circular shape similar to a cinnamon roll. Place into three large cake pans. Cover it and allow them to rise again for 30 minutes to an hour.
7. After this time, place them into the oven to bake at 350 degrees F for 30 to 45 minutes. Take and allow them to cool for 5 to 10 minutes before slicing and serving.

EASTER CAKE

Preparation time: 10 minutes

Cooking time: 40 minutes

Servings: 5

Ingredients

- ½ cup golden raisins
- One small cup or bowl of warm water or rum
- ½ cup warm milk (between 98° F and 105° F)
- Two teaspoons of instant yeast
- ½ cup sugar
- Five egg yolks
- Two teaspoons vanilla extract
- Two teaspoons almond extract
- 2 cups all-purpose flour, sifted
- ¼ teaspoon of salt
- ½ cup of melted, unsalted butter
- One teaspoon lemon zest
- ½ cup candied orange peel (optional)
- ⅓ cup chopped almonds (optional)
- Glaze (optional)

- One ¼ cups confectioners' sugar, sifted
- ¼ cup lemon juice

Directions

1. Prepare the Babka
2. Soak the raisins with hot water (or rum) to plump them up.
3. In a separate bowl, add the yeast to the lukewarm milk. Set aside.
4. Using a stand mixer with a paddle attachment. You can also use a stand mixer with beaters. Add the sugar and egg yolks to the mixer bowl and beat until thick and lemon-colored (usually 3 to 5 minutes). Add the almond extract and vanilla extract to the egg mixture and combine well.
5. Add the milk and yeast mixture to the egg mixture and mix until combined.
6. Drain the raisins and set them aside.
7. Add the salt and flour to a separate bowl and mix until combined.
8. Add 1 cup of flour and salt to the egg and yeast mixture in your standing mixer bowl. Mix using the paddle attachment until well incorporated.
9. Add the second cup of the flour and salt mixture and beat vigorously for about 5 to 7 minutes.
10. Add melted butter to the bowl and beat an additional 7 to 10 minutes.
11. Beat lemon zest, candied orange peel, and almonds in the raisins. Scrape down the sides of the bowl. The dough should be sticky. Cover the bowl using a clean, damp towel. Put the bowl in a warm place and let rise until doubled in size.
12. Generously butter a Bundt cake pan. You can also use a traditional babka pan or a kugelhopf pan.
13. Transfer the risen dough to the greased pan.
14. Cover with a clean, damp towel and let rise one more hour or until dough almost fills the pan.
15. Preheating the oven to 350° F and bake the Babka for 45–50 minutes, or when a toothpick can be inserted into the centre comes out clean. The Babka should be golden brown.
16. Cool for 5 minutes in the pan. Moving onto a cooling rack until completely cool.
17. Prepare the Glaze
18. Put confectioners' sugar in a medium bowl.
19. Mix the lemon juice one teaspoon at a time until you get the desired consistency. The glaze should be thick but pourable.
20. Complete the Babka
21. Sprinkle the glaze over the top of the Babka.
22. Chill if desired.
23. Serve and enjoy!

Notes: If you like, you can substitute 1/4 cup rum for the lemon juice for the glaze.

HONEY SPICE CAKE

Preparation time: 10 minutes

Cooking time: 50 minutes

Servings: 4

All ingredients should be at room temperature

Spice Ingredients

- 2 Tablespoons ground cinnamon
- 1 Tablespoon ground cardamom
- 1 Tablespoon ground black pepper
- 1 Tablespoon ground nutmeg
- ⅓ Tablespoons ground cloves
- ½ Tablespoons ground aniseed
- 1 Tablespoon ground ginger

Cake Ingredients

- 1 cup dark honey
- ¼ cup packed dark brown sugar
- 3 ½ Tablespoons unsalted butter
- 2 Tablespoons spices, divided
- 1 Tablespoon orange zest
- Two eggs
- 1 ½ teaspoons baking powder
- 2 cups all-purpose flour, sifted

Directions

1. Prepare Spice Mixture Mix all of the spices in a small bowl. Pour the mixture into an airtight jar or container. You'll have enough spices for more than one cake.
2. Prepare Cake Mixture
3. Preheat oven to 350° F.
4. Butter a 9" fluted cake pan and then line it with parchment paper. Using a pastry brush to apply butter to the parchment paper.
5. Combine the honey, brown sugar, butter, and one tablespoon of spices in a medium saucepan. Add in the orange zest. Heat the mixture over low heat. Mix with a wooden spoon until the mixture is smooth. Take off the burner and cool for 10 minutes.
6. Using a small bowl, beat the eggs lightly.
7. Add the beaten eggs to the cooled honey and sugar mixture.
8. Using a large mixing bowl, sift the flour and baking powder.
9. Add one tablespoon of the spice mixture to the bowl.
10. Add the flour mixture to the honey mixture and beat well. You can use a wooden spoon or a mixer. The final batter should be thick and smooth.
11. Pour the batter into your prepared pan.
12. Bake in the preheated oven for 1 hour.
13. Remove the cake from the oven and let it cool.
14. You can eat the cake as soon as it's cooled. You can also wrap it in tinfoil, put it in an airtight plastic bag, and let the spices intensify.

Toppings You can sprinkle Polish Spice Cake with powdered sugar. You can also apply chocolate icing or glaze. (See the Glazes, Icing, & Spice Mix section for topping recipes).

POLISH DOUGHNUTS

Preparation time: 10 minutes

Cooking time: 40 minutes

Servings: 4

Ingredients

- 12 egg yolks
- One teaspoon salt
- Two packets of active dry yeast
- ¼ cup water heated to 105°
- ⅓ cup unsalted butter, room temperature
- ½ cup granulated sugar
- 1 cup heavy whipping cream
- ½ teaspoon nutmeg
- One teaspoon pure vanilla extract
- zest of 1 orange
- 3 Tablespoons rum or brandy
- 4 cups all-purpose flour, sifted
- 3 Tablespoons melted butter (optional)
- 1 cup granulated sugar (optional)

Directions

1. Beat 12 egg yolks with the salt in a medium bowl at high speed until thick. Set aside.
2. In the standing mixer, dissolve two packets of dry yeast in 1/4 cup water that is 105° F. Wait for about 5 minutes until the mixture is foamy.
3. Cream the granulated sugar and butter in a separate bowl until fluffy and beat into the yeast mixture.
4. Scald 1 cup whipping cream and cool to lukewarm.
5. Add the nutmeg, vanilla extract, and orange zest to the lukewarm whipping cream.
6. Add the lukewarm cream, rum or brandy, egg yolks, and flour to the yeast mixture.
7. Use a dough hook attachment to mix the dough quickly until the ingredients are combined.
8. Increase the speed to medium-high and mix for 5 to 10 minutes until the dough is nice and elastic and has pulled away from the sides of the mixing bowl.
9. Transfer the dough to a large, greased bowl.
10. Cover the mixing bowl using a plastic wrap or clean towel and put it in a warm spot until it doubles in size.
11. Punch the dough down and knead. Make the dough into a rounded shape and return it to the bowl. Cover the bowl with a clean towel or plastic wrap and allow it to double in size again.
12. Roll the dough on a floured surface until it's 3/4" thick.
13. Use a 3" biscuit cutter to cut out 3" rounds. If you have a 3" glass, you can use that too. Combine any scrap dough, roll it out, and cut out more rounds.
14. Put the rounds on parchment paper-lined baking sheets. Make sure there's some space between the rounds. Cover the baking sheets with plastic wrap. Put the baking sheets in a warm place and wait for the rounds to double in size. This can take 30 minutes or longer.
15. Pour 2-inches of oil into a heavy-bottomed pot. Since the oil temperature is critical, use a deep-fry thermometer with a clip and attach it to the pot so that the probe is in the oil.

16. Heat the oil to 350°F.
17. When the oil reaches 350°F, use a large, heat-resistant slotted spatula or spoon to slide up to 3 paczkis at a time into the oil. One important secret is to put the dry side of the paczki, which is the side that was on top when the paczki was rising on the baking sheet, face down in the oil. This will help them increase nicely.
18. Cook for 3 minutes or until the bottoms are golden brown. Use the spatula to flip each paczki over carefully. Try not to splash the oil or cut into the paczki dough—Cook for three more minutes or until nicely browned.
19. Transfer the fried pączki to absorbent paper, layers of paper towels, or brown paper bags.
20. If you want to top your paczki with granulated sugar, then first put a cup of granulated sugar in a soft plastic bag. The bags you get at the supermarket are perfect.
21. Brush the tops and sides of each warm paczki with melted butter. Put each paczki in the bag and shake it to coat with the sugar. Take the paczki out of the bag, shake off any loose sugar, and set it aside to cool.
22. After the paczki has cooled, you can add the filling.

Add the Filling, and Paczki fillings are usually fruit-based. Raspberry preserves, strawberry preserves, cherry preserves, blueberry preserves, apricot preserves, and apple preserves are all familiar. Prune preserves are very popular with some families. Rose petal jam is a traditional filling. Lemon curd and custard are delicious fillings.

When I make paczki, I like to add the filling after the paczki has been fried. I add the filling to a pastry bag and use a plain, rounded tip. I insert the end into the side of each paczki and squeeze in about 1-1/2 teaspoons of filling. That's it! I think it's easier to add the filling after the paczki has been fried and cooled.

However, there are two other ways to add filling:

The first is to put some fruit filling on an unbaked dough round. Fold the edge of the dough up and over the filling. Pinch and seal the edges with water. Then roll the dough ball gently in your hands like a snowball to get an excellent, round shape. Place the dough on a parchment paper-lined baking pan. After you've filled all the uncooked paczki and they're on the baking pan, cover the pan with a clean towel or plastic wrap. Place the baking pan in a warm place and allow the dough to rise (approximately 30 minutes).

The second way is to put some filling in the center of a dough round. Then put a second dough round on top of it. Seal the edges with water. Roll each dough ball i hands gently to get a rounded shape. Put all the filled dough on a parchment paper-lined baking pan and cover with a clean towel or plastic wrap. Move the baking pan in a warm place and allow the dough to rise (approximately 30 minutes).

Adding the Topping There are several different types of toppings used for paczki:

Granulated Sugar. As I mentioned earlier, I like to apply this topping when the paczki is still warm before adding the filling.

Powdered Sugar. This is probably my favorite topping. I wait until the paczki is cooled and the filling has been added. Then I dust each paczki with powdered sugar.

Glaze. You can also make a simple vanilla or chocolate glaze. It's easy to dip the very top of the paczki in the glaze, shake off the excess, and place it on a rack in a baking pan to catch any drips. Candied orange peel on top of a glazed paczki is delicious.

CLASSIC LAZANKI WITH BEEF AND MUSHROOMS

Preparation time: 10 minutes

Cooking time: 50 minutes

Servings: 4

Ingredients:

- 2 tbsp. extra virgin olive oil
- 10 tbsp. butter, divided
- 1 pound of cremini mushrooms, sliced
- 1 pound of ground beef
- 3 cups of onions, diced
- 2 pounds of green cabbage, cored and shredded
- 1 tbsp. caraway seeds
- 1 ½ cups of sauerkraut, drained well
- One bay leaf
- 1 ½ tsp. dried thyme
- ½ tsp. dried marjoram
- 1 tsp. paprika
- ½ tsp. salt
- ¼ tsp. ground black pepper
- 1 cup of sour cream, divided
- 1 12 Ounce bag of egg noodles
- ¼ cup of fresh parsley chopped

Directions:

1. Place a large skillet over high heat. Add in the olive oil and butter. Once the butter is melted, add in the mushrooms—Cook for 10 minutes or until soft. Transfer the mushrooms into a medium bowl.
2. Add in two more tablespoons of butter and once the butter is melted, add in the beef. Cook for 3-4 minutes or until the meat is no longer pink in color. Transfer to the bowl with the mushrooms.
3. Add in two more tablespoons of butter. Once melted, add in the onions and cook for 5 minutes or until the onions are caramelized. Move the onions to the side and add the cabbage and caraway seeds. Continue to cook for 5 minutes before mixing with the onions.
4. Add the cooked mushrooms and beef back into the skillet. Add in the remaining butter, drained sauerkraut, bay leaf, marjoram, paprika, a dash of salt, black pepper, and ½ cup of sour cream. Stir to mix evenly.
5. Cook until the mixture begins to bubble. Once bubbling, reduce the heat to low and cook for 45 minutes while uncovered.
6. Remove from the heat after this time and toss out the bay leaf.
7. While this mixture is cooking, prepare the egg noodles according to the directions on the package.
8. Once the noodles are cooked, place them into large serving bowls. Top the noodles off with the Lazanki mixture and serve with a dollop of sour cream and a garnish of parsley.

POLISH VANILLA CUSTARD SLICE

Preparation time: 10 minutes

Cooking time: 40 minutes

Servings: 4

Ingredients for the Choux Pastry:

- 2 tbsp. unsalted butter
- 1 cup of all-purpose flour
- 1 cup of water
- Five large eggs

Ingredients for the Vanilla Custard Cream:

- Three ¼ cups of vanilla custard
- Two large eggs
- 2 tbsp. pure vanilla extract
- 4 tbsp. all-purpose flour
- 2 tbsp. cornflour
- One ¼ cup of heavy cream

Ingredient for Serving:

- A dusting of confectioner's sugar

Directions:

1. Begin with preheating your oven to 425 degrees F.
2. While the oven is heating up, make the choux pastry. To do this, use a medium saucepan and add in the water and butter. Set over medium heat and bring this mixture to a boil. Once boiling, add in the all-purpose flour and stir thoroughly until a ball of dough forms. Transfer this dough into a large bowl and add in the eggs. Stir until smooth.
3. Grease a large baking sheet with a touch of butter. Spread the dough onto the baking sheet and roll until ⅛ inch in thickness.
4. Place into the oven to bake for 25 minutes. Remove after this time and allow it to cool.
5. Meanwhile, make the vanilla custard cream. To do this, add the heavy cream into a large bowl. Beat with an electric mixer until peaks begin to form.
6. Then, place a large saucepan over medium heat. Add the custard, large eggs, all-purpose flour, and pure vanilla. Whisk until smooth in consistency. Set over low heat and cook for 5 minutes or until the custard is thick. Add in the whipped cream and whisk to incorporate. Remove from the heat.
7. Cut the freshly baked pastry in half. Spread the custard cream over the top. Cut into squares and serve.

CABBAGE CUCUMBER RADISH SALAD

Preparation time: 10 minutes

Cooking time: 0 minutes

Servings: 4

Ingredients:

- ½ a head of cabbage, roughly chopped
- One bunch of radishes
- ½ an English cucumber, thinly sliced

- A handful of dill, fresh, and roughly chopped
- ¾ to 1 cup of mayonnaise
- Dash of salt and black pepper

Directions:

1. Add all the ingredients into a large bowl.
2. Toss thoroughly to mix evenly.
3. Season with additional salt and black pepper.
4. Place into the fridge to chill until you are ready to serve.

SAUCY RED POTATO GOULASH

Preparation time: 10 minutes

Cooking time: 30 minutes

Servings: 4

Ingredients:

- Touch of extra virgin olive oil
- 1 14 ounces smoked sausage, sliced into medallions
- 2 tbsp. butter
- Two onions, cut into quarters, and thinly sliced
- One clove of garlic, pressed
- Dash of salt
- ¾ tsp. black pepper
- 1 ½ tsp. paprika
- Ten red potatoes, peeled and sliced into ½ inch thick circles
- 1 ½ cup of chicken stock
- 1 tbsp. of flat-leaf parsley, chopped

Directions:

1. First place a large skillet over medium to high heat. Add in the olive oil and once the oil is hot, add in the sausage. Cook for 10-15 minutes or until the sausage begins to caramelize. Remove from the skillet and set aside.
2. Using the same skillet, add in the butter. Once melted, add in the onions. Cook for 5 to 7 minutes or until the onions caramelize. Add garlic and season with salt and black pepper. Cook for an additional 1 to 2 minutes or until the garlic is aromatic.
3. Add in the sliced potatoes and toss to mix. Add in the chicken stock and cover. Cook for 15 minutes before removing the cover. Continue to simmer for 10 minutes or until the potatoes are tender.
4. Add the smoked sausage back into the skillet as well as the parsley. Spray a bit of olive oil over the top and stir to mix—season with salt and black pepper.
5. Remove from the heat and serve.

POLISH COTTAGE CHEESE NOODLE RECIPE

Preparation time: 10 minutes

Cooking time: 40 minutes

Servings: 4

Ingredients

- 1 (16 ounces) package cottage cheese
- 1/2 cup almond butter
- 1/2 cup sour cream
- 1/2 teaspoon salt
- One red onion
- 1 (16 ounces) package noodles
- 1/4 teaspoon black pepper

Directions

1. First peel the onion and chop it finely.
2. In a pan, melt the almond butter and fry the onion for 5 minutes.
3. In another pot, boil some water with salt.
4. Cook the noodles for 8 minutes, and drain once tender.
5. Transfer the noodles into a bowl.
6. Add the onion, sour cream, cottage cheese and mix gently.
7. Season using salt and black pepper.
8. Heat the mixture for eight more minutes and serve hot.

POLISH CHICKEN AND DUMPLINGS

Preparation time: 10 minutes

Cooking time: 30 minutes

Servings: 4

Ingredients:

- 3 pounds chicken
- One onion
- 1 celery stalk
- 1 tsp. dried basil
- ½ tsp. salt
- 1 tsp. black pepper
- 1 10.75-oz. can of condensed cream chicken soup
- Four eggs
- 2 tbsp. olive oil
- 4 cups flour
- 2 cups water

Directions:

1. Take a large pot and add chicken, celery, and onion before filling it with water.
2. Now add basil, salt, pepper, poultry seasoning, and a little salt. Bring it to a boil.
3. Simmer for 2 hours until the chicken is done.

4. Remove the chicken from the broth and strain it to remove seasonings.
5. Add the cream of chicken soup after transferring the broth to a pan to simmer. Then allow the chicken to cool down.
6. Take a bowl and in it combine the olive oil, salt, eggs, pepper, and also 2 cups of water. Slowly add flour to it as you stir.
7. Take a spoonful of dough and cut little pieces into the broth.
8. Then cover and simmer for approximately 15 minutes.
9. Then cut the chicken into small pieces before adding it to broth and heating.
10. When done, serve.

HAM SALAD FOR SANDWICHES

Preparation time: 10 minutes

Cooking time: 0 minutes

Servings: 4

Ingredients:

- ¼ cups mayonnaise
- 3 tbsp. crushed onions
- ½ lb. ham
- 2 tsp. Worcestershire sauce
- Six white bread slices

Directions:

1. Begin by mixing all the ingredients in a bowl.
2. Then refrigerate the mixture before sandwiching the mix between two slices of bread.
3. Serve and enjoy!

EASY POLISH NOODLES

Preparation time: 10 minutes

Cooking time: 50 minutes

Servings: 4

Ingredients:

- One 49.5-fl. Oz. can chicken broth
- ½ cup water
- 1 tbsp. chicken soup base
- 1 16-oz. package kluski noodles

Directions:

1. Take a 6-quart saucepan and add chicken broth, chicken base, and water.
2. Then allow it to boil.

3. Add kluski noodles, then reduce heat and simmer for 30-40 minutes until the liquid is completely absorbed.

POLISH SUMMER BORSHCH

Preparation time: 10 minutes

Cooking time: 30 minutes

Servings: 4

Ingredients:

- 2 tbsp. flour
- Two dill pickles
- 4 cups beef broth
- ¼ cup water
- One lb. canned beet
- One cup sour cream
- ½ tsp. sugar
- 1 cup brine
- 2 tbsp. chopped green onions
- Salt to taste
- Four boiled eggs
- 1 tbsp. chopped dill

Directions:

1. Take a big pot and add into it the broth, beet liquid, and also the beets. Then, heat it.
2. Next, mix the water and the flour and bring it to a boil.
3. Let it cool. Then, except for the eggs, combine all of the remaining ingredients in a mixing bowl.
4. Refrigerate it before topping with chopped eggs and serve.

SAUSAGE AND LENTILS

Preparation time: 10 minutes

Cooking time: 20 minutes

Servings: 4

Ingredients:

- ½ cup chopped onion
- 3 cups water
- 1 cup dried lentils
- 1 tsp. ground cumin
- 1 8-oz. pack kielbasa or Polish sausage
- 1 tsp. ground cumin
- Salt and pepper to taste

Directions:

1. Take a saucepan, add lentils, onion, and water, and heat at a medium heat.
2. Rise it to a boil and cook it for 15 minutes.
3. Add sliced sausages and season with salt, cumin, and pepper.
4. Simmer until the lentils turn tender. This should be about 5 to 12 minutes.
5. When done, serve right away.

CHEESECAKE

Preparation time: 10 minutes

Cooking time: 40 minutes

Servings: 4

Ingredients Crust

- ½ cup sugar
- 2 cups all-purpose flour, sifted
- ¾ teaspoon baking powder
- 5 ounces cold unsalted butter
- Two large egg yolks (at room temperature)
- 3 Tablespoons sour cream

Filling

- 2 cups sugar
- 5 ounces unsalted butter (at room temperature)
- Four large eggs separated (at room temperature)
- One vanilla
- 1 Tablespoon grated lemon peel
- 1 ounce rum (optional)
- 2 pounds farmer's cheese
- ½ cup raisins

Directions

1. Prepare the Crust

2. In a food processor, mix the sugar, flour, and baking soda—pulse in the cold butter.
3. In a bowl, mix the egg yolks and sour cream until combined.
4. Add the egg yolk-sour cream mixture to the flour-sugar mixture. Pulse until combined. Now if the dough is too dry, add the whole egg and pulse again until combined.
5. Grease a 13" x 9" baking pan or a 10" springform pan with butter.
6. Roll the dough out so that it's big enough to line the bottom of the pan and up the sides. If using a springform pan, line the bottom of the pan and halfway up the sides of the pan.
7. Prepare the Filling
8. Preheat the oven to 350°F
9. dip the raisins in hot water for 10 minutes until they plump up. Drain the water and set the raisins aside.
10. Cream the sugar with the room temperature butter in a large bowl until the mixture is fluffy.
11. Beat in the four-room temperature egg yolks, the vanilla, grated lemon peel the rum (if using), and the raisins (if using) until well blended.
12. Blend the 2 pounds of farmer's cheese in a food processor or blender until smooth.
13. Add the blended farmer's cheese to the egg yolk mixture and mix until thoroughly combined.
14. Beat the four large egg whites in a separate bowl until they form stiff peaks.
15. Fold the egg whites into the cheese mixture.
16. Pour the mixture over the pastry dough in the baking or springform pan.
17. Bake the cheesecake for 50 to 60 minutes. The top should be lightly brown, and the filling should be set. Take care not to burn the top.
18. Remove from the oven and cool completely. Chill in the refrigerator before serving.

ALMOND AND HONEY THINS

Preparation time: 10 minutes

Cooking time: 50 minutes

Servings: 5

All ingredients should be at room temperature

- 8 cups almonds, blanched
- 1 cup cold water
- 1 cup sugar
- 1 cup honey

Directions

1. Coarsely chop the almonds
2. Bring the cold water and sugar to a boil in a large pot over medium-high heat.
3. Turn down the heat to low and stir continuously for 3 to 5 minutes until the sugar completely dissolves and clear the mixture. The longer you cook the mix, the thicker the syrup will be. If you take a small amount of syrup in a spoon and see any sugar crystals, cook it a bit longer.
4. Add the chopped almonds to the syrup and simmer until the syrup brown.
5. Add the honey to the mixture and simmer for 1/2 hour. Stir the mixture with a wooden spoon.
6. Pour a portion of the mixture on a cold, flat surface. My Grandmother used her kitchen tabletop. You can also use a silicone baking sheet.

7. Roll the mixture into a thin sheet using a wooden rolling pin moistened with water or oil.
8. Allow to cool and then cut in diagonal stripes.
9. Repeat the process for the remaining honey almond mixture.
10. Store in an airtight container.

APPLE BANANA CUPCAKES

Preparation time: 10 minutes

Cooking time: 30 minutes

Servings: 4

Ingredients:

- 2 cups all-purpose flour
- 1 tsp. baking soda
- 1 tsp. salt
- 1/2 tsp. ground cinnamon
- 1/2 tsp. ground nutmeg
- 2/3 cup shortening
- 1 1/4 cups white sugar
- Two eggs
- 1 tsp. vanilla extract
- 1/4 cup buttermilk
- 1 cup ripe bananas, mashed
- Two apples - peeled, cored, and shredded

Directions:

1. The first step is to preheat the oven to 190 degrees C/375 degrees F. Grease then flour or put paper liners on 24 muffin cups. Sift nutmeg, cinnamon, salt, baking soda, and flour together. Put aside.
2. Cream the sugar and shortening in a big bowl until fluffy and light. One at a time beat eggs in. Mix in buttermilk and vanilla. Beat flour mixture in, mixing until just incorporated. Fold in shredded apples and mashed bananas. Fill every muffin cup to half full.
3. Bake for about 20-25 minutes in preheated oven until an inserted toothpick in the middle exits clean. Cool.

ALMOND CRESCENT COOKIES

Preparation time: 10 minutes

Cooking time: 30 minutes

Servings: 5

Ingredients

- 8 ounces unsalted butter at room temperature
- ½ cup sugar
- One teaspoon vanilla extract
- One large egg yolk, at room temperature

- ¼ cup ground, blanched almonds
- One ⅔ cups all-purpose flour sifted
- Powdered sugar

Directions

1. Preheat oven to 350° F.
2. Cream the sugar and butter in a large bowl until the mixture is fluffy.
3. Beat in the vanilla extract and egg yolk until well-mixed.
4. Using hand mixer or stand mixer to gradually mix the ground almonds and the all-purpose flour until incorporated.
5. redo until all of the dough is used:
6. Take a heaping tablespoon of dough. Shape it into a 2-1/2" to 3" log that's thicker in the middle than at the ends. Then bend it into a crescent and put it on a parchment-lined cookie sheet.
7. Bake the cookies for 20 minutes or until light brown. Remove from the oven.
8. Pour some powdered sugar into a shallow bowl.
9. Roll the warm crescents in the powdered sugar. Cool the cookies on racks.

ANGEL WING COOKIES

Preparation time: 10 minutes

Cooking time: 20 minutes

Servings: 6

Ingredients

- Six egg yolks at room temperature
- Pinch of salt
- 4 Tablespoons granulated sugar
- One teaspoon vanilla
- 4 Tablespoons sour cream
- One teaspoon lemon zest
- 2 Tablespoons vodka
- 1-1/2 cups all-purpose flour
- 1 quart of oil for frying (canola or safflower)
- 1 cup confectioner's sugar

Directions

1. Beat the egg yolks, salt, and granulated sugar with a hand mixer until thick and lemon yellow in a large bowl.
2. Add the vanilla, sour cream, lemon zest, and vodka to the bowl and mix until blended.
3. Now gradually add the flour to the mixture until the dough is firm. Mix with a paddle attachment for 3 to 5 minutes.
4. If you don't have a paddle attachment, turn the dough onto a floured surface and knead with your hands for 3 minutes.
5. Now place the dough in a bowl and cover with a clean towel. Allow the dough to rest for one hour.
6. Move the dough out on a floured surface. Roll the dough out until it's fragile. Cut 2" x 7" strips.
7. Cut a 2-1/2" vertical slot in each strip

8. Take one end of the strip through the slit. Gently pull both ends of the strip. It will look a bit like a bow tie.
9. Heat oil in a deep fryer to 350° F. Add 4-5 strips to the oil and deep fry until each side is golden brown.
10. Move from the oil and drain on paper towels. Cool.
11. Sprinkle liberally with confectioner's sugar.

BUTTER COOKIES WITH JAM

Preparation time: 10 minutes

Cooking time: 50 minutes

Servings: 6

Ingredients

- 8 ounces softened butter
- ½ cup sugar
- Two large egg yolks at room temperature
- One teaspoon vanilla
- 2 cups all-purpose flour
- ½ teaspoon baking powder
- ¼ teaspoon salt
- 10 Tablespoons Jam (any flavor)

Directions

1. Using a large bowl mix the butter and sugar together until they're light and fluffy.
2. Beat in the egg yolks and vanilla until all the ingredients are combined.
3. Now gently mix the flour, baking powder, and salt to the bowl, beating with a mixer until the dry ingredients are incorporated.
4. Fridge the bowl for 1 hour, covered with plastic wrap.
5. Preheat oven to 350° F.
6. Line baking sheets with parchment paper.
7. redo until all of the dough is used:
8. Use a spoon to scoop out dough, roll it into a ball, and put it on the cookie sheet. Flatten the ball gently.
9. Using finger to make a depression in the center of the cookie.
10. Fill the depression with ½ teaspoon jam.
11. Bake cookies for 8-10 minutes until the edges are lightly brown.
12. Remove from the oven and cool the cookies on a cooling rack.
13. Store cookies in an airtight container.

CAT'S EYE SANDWICH COOKIES

Preparation time: 10 minutes

Cooking time: 60 minutes

Servings: 3

- Ingredients
- 3 cups all-purpose flour, sifted
- ½ pound cold butter, cubed
- 2 Tablespoons vanilla sugar **
- 1 cup sour cream
- Jam
- Powdered sugar

Directions

1. Put the flour into a large bowl. Mash the butter cubes into the flour until the flour looks like small peas. I use a pastry cutter but also a food processor.
2. Add the vanilla sugar and sour cream to the flour-butter mixture. Quickly work the mixture into a dough.
3. Fridge the dough for 2 to 3 hours, wrapped in plastic wrap.
4. Preheat oven to 350° F.
5. Take the dough out of the frigde and turn it onto a floured surface.
6. Roll the dough out to a ¼ inch thickness. By using a round cookie cutter to cut out raw cookies. (You can use a flower-shaped cookie cutter or other shapes too. Use the same form for all of the cookies.)
7. After cutting out all of the dough circles, divide them into two even groups.
8. Using a smaller, round cookie cutter to cut the center out of the first dough circles.
9. Take the scrap dough, combine it, and roll it out. Cut out more dough rounds. Cut the center out of half of these dough rounds.
10. Line baking sheets with parchment paper.
11. Place the dough rounds on the cookie sheets. Leave 1 inch between each dough round. Prick each dough round several times with a fork.
12. Bake for 10-15 minutes or until the edges of the cookies are lightly brown. Take the cookies out and repeat until all of the cookies have been baked.
13. Cool the cookies completely.
14. Spread a thin layer of jam on the cookies without holes in them.
15. Sprinkle powdered sugar on the cookies with holes in them.
16. Place a cookie (powdered sugar side up) on top of a cookie with the jam facing up. Press them together. Repeat for all of the cookies.
17. Store in an airtight container.

CINNAMON COOKIES

Preparation time: 10 minutes

Cooking time: 30 minutes

Servings: 6

Ingredients

- 2-1/2 cups flour
- ½ teaspoon baking soda
- 1-1/2 sticks of unsalted butter, at room temperature
- 1 cup sugar

- Zest of 1 lemon
- One teaspoon vanilla
- 1-1/4 teaspoons ground cinnamon
- Two eggs at room temperature
- One egg yolk beat with 1 Tablespoon water

Directions

1. In a medium bowl, mix the flour and the baking soda.
2. Cream the butter and sugar together in a large bowl. Add the lemon zest, vanilla, cinnamon, and the eggs and mix until smooth.
3. To the butter mixture add the flour mixture. Mix until you have a stiff dough.
4. Form the dough into a ball, wrap in plastic wrap, and refrigerate overnight.
5. On the next day heat the oven to 350° F.
6. Line a cookie sheet with parchment paper.
7. Roll out the dough to a ¼ inch thickness on a floured surface. Use a cookie cutter to cut the shapes you want.
8. Put the cookies on the cookie sheet, leaving the cookies an inch apart.
9. Brush each cookie with the egg yolk and water mixture.
10. Bake the cookies for about 15 minutes or until they turn golden.
11. Cool the cookies on a cooling rack.
12. Store in an airtight container.

PLUM CAKE

Preparation time: 20min
Cooking time: 40min

Servings: 7

Ingredients:

- 3 Eggs
- ½ cup of Sugar
- ½ cup softened Butter
- 1 tsp. of Lemon zest
- 2 cups of flour
- 2 tbsp. Sour cream
- ½ tsp. baking powder
- 1 tsp. Vanilla extract
- 1 ½ lb. Plums, fresh, cut in fours

Directions:

1. Preheat oven, 375F.
2. Separate the whites from the yolks and mash them in separate bowls.
3. In another bowl, combine the baking powder and flour. Transfer the flour into the yolk and blend well. Fold in the whites.
4. In a previously greased pan (or with parchment paper), spread the mixed batter. Arrange the plums on the batter with their skin down.
5. Bake for 40 minutes. Set aside to cool.

6. Top with plum sauce or powdered sugar (or both) and serve. Enjoy!

JEWISH CHALLAH

Preparation time: 10 minutes

Cooking time: 30 minutes

Servings: 4

Ingredients:

- Eight teaspoons of active yeast
- Two tablespoons of sugar
- 5 cups of water
- One and a half cups of honey
- Two tablespoons of salt
- One and quarter cups of oil
- One egg
- 2.2kg all-purpose flour

Topping:

- 1 cup of flour
- 1 cup of sugar
- Half a cup of olive oil
- One teaspoon of vanilla extract

Directions:

1. Mix 1 cup of water, sugar, and yeast. When it bubbles, add honey, salt oil, and egg. Mix it well.
2. Add remaining water and flour. Make dough. Let dough rise for 2 hours.
3. Split the dough into six pieces and that six into six smaller ones. And braid challahs.
4. Let challah rise for 20 minutes. Brush them with egg wash.
5. Bake challahs for 45 minutes at 180°C.
6. Mix all topping ingredients and sprinkle the mixture over challahs.
7. Serve cooled.

KISSEL

Preparation time: 10 minutes

Cooking time: 30 minutes

Servings: 4

Ingredients:

- 400g crushed strawberries
- 1 cup water
- 1/2 cup sugar

- Three tablespoons potato starch
- Four tablespoons cornstarch
- 1/2 cup cold water

Directions:

1. In a large saucepan, add 1 cup of water and sugar to boil. Then remove it from heat.
2. Dissolve the potato starch into 1/2 cup cold water and then stir this into the sugar-water mixture. Next, return it to the heat and bring to a boil while stirring constantly in the process. Add strawberries in and then mix well.
3. Portion bowl that has been rinsed with cold water and then put it in the refrigerator until it is firm. This should take about 3 hours. When ready to serve, do so with your preference of cream, half-and-half, milk, or whipped cream.

MAKOVEC

Preparation time: 10 minutes

Cooking time: 30 minutes

Servings: 4

Ingredients:

- 30g yeast
- 320g flour
- Four tablespoons of sugar
- 1/4 teaspoon of salt
- One tablespoon of strong alcohol
- 3/4 teaspoon of vanilla extract
- Four egg yolks
- 120ml milk
- 100g butter

Filling:

- 330g poppy seeds
- 112g light brown sugar
- 65g raisins
- 33g walnuts, chopped
- Two tablespoons of honey
- One teaspoon of almond extract
- 1/2 teaspoons of cinnamon
- 1/2 tablespoons of butter,
- 1/3 cup of candied orange zest
- Four egg whites

Directions:

1. Mix yeast with one tablespoon of sugar. Add two tablespoons of flour and all milk, stir and leave aside for 20-30 minutes.

2. Add remaining flour, alcohol, vanilla extract, egg yolks, and milk and knead until well combined (around 5-10 minutes).
3. Add melted butter and knead until well mixed. Cover the dough with a towel and allow it to rise somewhere warm for about an hour.
4. Filling: Place the poppy seeds in a bowl and pour hot boiling water over them and then leave it to cool. Remove the water and ground the seeds in a coffee grinder twice.
5. Add and mix well the following ingredients: sugar, raisins, walnuts, honey, almond extract, cinnamon, butter, and candied orange zest.
6. Then, in a separate dish, mash the egg whites until stiff.
7. Add this into the poppy seed mixture and next gently fold it in.
8. Divide the dough in 2 parts and then roll each part on a floured surface.
9. Spread the filling onto each one of the rectangles.
10. Roll the dough into a roll shape, beginning with the long edge. Turn the ends under so that the filling will not leak out.
11. Bake rolls at 190°C for 40 minutes.
12. Leave them to cool. Serve.

FLAT CAKE

Preparation time: 10 minutes

Cooking time: 50 minutes

Servings: 4

Ingredients:

- 180g room-temperature butter
- Four tablespoons sugar
- 50g ground blanched almonds
- 1/2 teaspoon grated lemon zest
- 2 1/2 cups all-purpose flour
- Two large hard-cooked egg yolks sieved
- One sizeable raw egg yolk
- 180g apricot preserves
- 180g raspberry or cherry preserves
- Confectioners' sugar
- Pinch salt
- Pinch cinnamon

Directions:

1. Mix sugar and butter using an electric mixer until it is light and fluffy. By hand, stir in almonds, zest, flour, measure flour correctly, and hard-cooked egg yolks.
2. Add the egg yolk, salt, and cinnamon, and then mix everything into a smooth dough. You can also do this in a food processor if you like.
3. Place the dough in plastic wrap and put it in the refrigerate for 30 minutes or more.
4. Heat oven to 180°C.

5. Cut off one-third of the dough and return it to the refrigerator. Roll out abut two-third of the dough and place on a pan. Fork tines should be used to pierce the dough. I am using a pastry brush, egg wash (1 beaten egg with one teaspoon water) dough.
6. Roll remaining 1/3 dough and cut into strips. Arrange strips lattice-style over dough. Brush lattice strips with egg wash. Bake this for 20 to 30 minutes, or until it is golden-brown and crisp.
7. Place the pastry on a plate and spoon the fruit preserve alternately into the open spaces of the latticework. Sprinkle lightly with confectioners' sugar. Allow cooling completely.

CONCLUSION

Thank you for making it to the end of this cookbook. If you have had the chance to try homemade Polish food, you will know how good it is. Everything they serve is prepared from scratch and with love.

These recipes are the best because they make it simple to make delicious and nutritious meals. Even if you're not an experienced cook, you can still enjoy the results! Polish recipes are simply delicious when you add the proper spices and ingredients.

Polish recipes are tasty and healthy, nutritious, and beneficial. The vegetables and protein in Polish recipes make them energy-dense, while the whole grains make them high in fiber and vitamins. The result is a meal that will satisfy your hunger, keep you full for hours on end, and won't weigh you down or give you an upset tummy. It's also easy to prepare so that you can enjoy it at any time of day or evening.

Polish recipes are some of the best around. Their simple ingredients and proper technique can become an excellent addition to any kitchen.

Polish food is hearty and filling, and while there may be many people who swear the food is made up of nothing but potatoes and meat, it couldn't be any farther from the truth. Polish food has a fascinating history and comprises various cultural influences, making it one of the unique cuisines around. Most Polish meals are grains, dumplings, vegetables, noodles, meats, potatoes, and decadent desserts. They are well-rounded and form one of the most delicious cuisines that you can enjoy today.

You will learn how easy it is to put some of these dishes together and discover for yourself that many words are made up of more than just potatoes and meat. Inside are 25 of the most delicious Polish recipes that you will ever find and that will help you impress your family with an exotic and unique meal.

Learning how to make these recipes will be with you in life. They are unique and yet delicious. Even if you haven't tried homemade Polish dishes, you will be able to make them yourself and truly enjoy them.

When you start cooking these meals, make sure not to change the ingredients or the measurements. Ok, you can add more or less black pepper and salt, but don't experiment with the others if you want to get the actual traditional meal on your table.

It is time to try your hand at making your Polish-inspired recipes using your favorite ingredients and the knowledge you learned from making other authentic Polish dishes.

Good luck.

Made in United States
Troutdale, OR
05/27/2024

20161115R00097